ATTENTION SEEKER

DARCY MICHAEL

ATTENTION SEEKER

A NEURODIVERGENT COMEDIAN'S GUIDE
TO ~~SURVIVING~~ THRIVING WITH ADHD

First American Edition, 2026
Published in the United States by DK Publishing
1745 Broadway, 20th Floor, New York, NY 10019

The authorized representative in the EEA is Dorling Kindersley
Verlag GmbH. Arnulfstr. 124, 80636 Munich, Germany

Copyright © Busy Donkey Productions Inc.
DK, a Division of Penguin Random House LLC
25 26 27 28 29 10 9 8 7 6 5 4 3 2 1
001-348556-JAN2026

All rights reserved.
Without limiting the rights under the copyright reserved above, no part of this publication may be reproduced, stored in or introduced into a retrieval system, or transmitted, in any form, or by any means (electronic, mechanical, photocopying, recording, or otherwise), without the prior written permission of the copyright owner.

No part of this publication may be used or reproduced in any manner for the purpose of training artificial intelligence technologies or systems. In accordance with Article 4(3) of the DSM Directive 2019/790, DK expressly reserves this work from the text and data mining exception.

A catalog record for this book
is available from the Library of Congress.
ISBN 978-0-5939-6675-4

Jacket design and illustrations by Lindsay Dobbs
Author photograph by Tom Belding

DK books are available at special discounts when purchased in bulk for sales promotions, premiums, fundraising, or educational use. For details, contact SpecialSales@dk.com

Printed and bound in the United States of America

www.dk.com

Dedicated to my ever-so-patient husband Jeremy and our incredible daughter Grace—without you both, I'd be completely lost.

I mean that quite literally.
Thank you for always knowing where I parked the car.

To my mom and dad,
thank you for giving me a life that taught me to put love and joy first. But it's probably best you stop reading here.

To all my family, I'm sorry for taking over every family dinner, but thanks for being my favorite audience—I love all of you.
Some of you more than others.

And to my friends that I didn't mention in this book: you're welcome—congrats on having excellent lawyers.

Well played. Well played, indeed.

CONTENTS

Foreword   11

Important Terms   24

Introduction   29

1 **Where Does ADHD Come From?**   38
   A Portrait of the Artist as a Young Neurodivergent

2 **ADHD & Addiction**   60
   Drugs, Debt, and Dancing (Except No Dancing)

3 **ADHD & Family**   68
   The Day the Apples Took Flight

4 **ADHD & Love**   79
   How to Take It Slow When Your Mind Moves Fast, Fast, Fast

5 **ADHD & Courtship**   90
   The Courtship of Grace's Father(s)

6 **ADHD & Marriage**   97
   When I Was Your Age, We Had to Walk Uphill
   Both Ways to Get Gay-Married

7 **ADHD, Creativity & Rejection**   105
   Untitled Oprah Project

8 **ADHD & Physical Wellness**   118
   My Fat Accompli

9 **ADHD & Money**   131
   A Deficit?! In This Attention Economy?!

10 **ADHD & What's in Front of You**   141
   Has Anyone Seen My Object Permanence?
   I Swear I Just Had It!

11 **ADHD & Your Diagnosis**   150
   You Can't Spell "Diagnosis" Without "Know."
   Well, Actually You Can.

12 **ADHD & Rock Bottom** — 165
Darcy Goes to Church. God Is Watching Something Else.

13 **ADHD & the Road Not Taken** — 170
Plants Live in One Place, and a Star Feeds Them

14 **ADHD & Travel** — 175
The Whirled Tour

15 **ADHD & Household Pets** — 192
3:10 to Yuma Dog

16 **ADHD & Finding Your Bliss** — 200
COVID-EOS or How I Met Your Mothers

17 **ADHD & Hyper-Distraction** — 208
How Using My ADHD for Clout Paid Off and Can for You, Too! (Just Probably Not Literally)

18 **ADHD & (Over)commitment** — 218
The Tour Neurodiversity Built

19 **ADHD & the Household** — 228
Homo Is Where the Heart Is

20 **When Is the End Ever the End?** — 236

21 **The Truth of It All** — 240

Epilogue — 245
Afterword by Yuma Dog — 251
After Afterword — 253
Acknowledgments — 255

FOREWORD

BIG DYS ENERGY: YOU CAN'T SPELL EXECUTIVE DYSFUNCTION WITHOUT A BIG OL' D

Forgive me if this is too "foreword," but the publishers insisted I write one.

[Ed. note: This is not true. Darcy just wanted to work in that joke.]

Let me start with what I'm not going to do: the sin of homo-mission. I'm not going to tell you to read this book. Because if you know yourself as well as I know myself, telling me to do something is very simply a great way to ensure that I will never do it. It's probably why my dentist and I don't get along. (Which is a shame, because as my husband will tell you, I love it when cavities get filled.)

What I will do is tell you why I wrote it.

Why did I write this book ... sorry ... lost my train of thought for a second—somebody got chinchilla fur stuck in the jets of the atrium jacuzzi. Oh, how I do wish it could be more like the en suite jacuzzi, but you know what they say: if wishes were dishes, Greeks would throw them in celebration. Anyway, what were we talking about? Oh, right, why I wrote this book. Well, it wasn't for the money, I promise. I'm just not motivated by material things. Maybe crypto?

So—WHY THIS BOOK? Well shit, I'll do you one better: why any book?

Before Darcy and Jer, before Justin Bieber, before the Weeknd or Shania Twain, but a little bit after insulin, Canada gave the world a man named Marshall McLuhan. Perhaps you recall that name from your school days? After all, he's still so venerated in our big, cold country that the lead dog from *Paw Patrol* was named in his honor.

McLuhan was a brilliant and extremely butch intellectual best known for his observation that "the medium is the message." If he'd been born fifty years later, he probably would have tweeted it ... which I think is part of his point? Anyway, because it was the sixties, he wrote a whole book on the subject, called *The Medium Is the Massage*, which has become one of Canada's most famous typos. McLuhan thought it was funny and decided to keep it in. (He was both butch and whimsical!) I should probably admit now that this typo is how I ended up reading the book on a Puerto Vallarta beach vacation, because I just assumed that it was an erotic thriller about a psychic who does shiatsu. My furiously blue-balled review almost tore apart the Goodreads community.

So now likely you're wondering what Marshall McLuhan has to do with any of this. OH, I'M SORRY, DID THE BOOK YOU BOUGHT BY THE GUY WHO'S INTERNET-FAMOUS FOR HAVING ADHD VEER OFF ONTO A TANGENT FOR A LITTLE BIT?! WELL, I FEEL JUST TERRIBLE! DID YOUR BATHING SUIT ALSO GET WET AT THE POOL?! WERE YOU SURROUNDED BY HOMOSEXUALS AT THE *GOLDEN GIRLS* CONVENTION?! PLEASE TELL ME MORE ABOUT THE EASILY PREDICTABLE TRAVESTIES BY WHICH YOU HAVE BEEN INCONVENIENCED!

Like the man with the pencil sharpener fetish said when he took down his pants, here's the point: what McLuhan was trying to say, put in twenty-first-century terms, was that the platform on which we consume any particular bit of content says just as much to us as the content of that content does.

Or to put it another way: even though my husband and I were surprised as fuck when we found an audience of millions for our little internet videos about ADHD, I don't think Marshall McLuhan would have been. No, rather like the bellboy in Puerto Vallarta who didn't knock before bringing in a tray of slushy margaritas, McLuhan would have seen me and Jer coming.

Because making short videos for the internet about ADHD is like serving cheese on crackers that are also made of cheese. Combining the internet and ADHD is like breeding a new pedigree of dog by combining a male golden retriever with a female golden retriever. The internet and ADHD go together like [spends 94 minutes googling "Tom Selleck Burt Reynolds Marshall McLuhan no moustache"].

When my neurofabulous ass wandered out into the wilds of the internet, I found a home on a whole new, vogueing, pose-striking dance floor. Our fans could easily wrap their heads and hearts around the 60-second videos that Jer and I were making. And from a production standpoint, we felt equipped to make those videos, some of which could take upward of sixty-six or even seventy seconds of our time.

So then why a fucking book, Darcy? Why produce yet one more of the daunting, terrifying word-bricks in the bundle hanging precariously over the ADHD head? Why squeeze out one more of the giant stacks of pages that have been making us feel nervous and small ever since we were nervous and small?

"Oh Darcy, Darcy, why did you take this book deal?"

Here's the deal, my dearest sweet reader, and this is the truth: it's honestly because I think we can do it. And I want to prove it to us. A book isn't too much. I can write it. You can read it. We're gonna get through this book together and we're gonna grow from it.[1]

The fact is, I wanted to write a book because I wanted a chance to tell my ADHD story, the story of my family's life with neurodiversity, in a different way. Jer and I have been so lucky to get to share our journey with legions of online creeps in bite-size videos and with breathing, sweating, laughing, and clapping IRL audiences around the world at our live on-stage shows. But a book is different. One of the most popular metaphors for ADHD is an iceberg, which is ironic since the most famous iceberg ever doesn't appear until like two-and-a-half hours into a three-hour movie—so nobody with ADHD got to see it. We'll talk later about the ADHD iceberg (or skip to page 160), but what you need to know about icebergs for now is that they're notorious for showing way less on the surface than they have going on underneath.

I wrote this book because I wanted to show you the bottom of my iceberg. (Jer tried to make me delete that sentence because he said it sounded dirty—uh, why do you think I wrote it, buddy?!) My ADHD journey has been totally one-of-a-kind, just like everyone else's. But the special ways that neurodiversity has shaped my experiences—of falling in love; of coming out; of trying to make it in show business; of trying to make peace with food and my body; of building a life with the man of my dreams, despite obstacles as daunting as homophobia or a chin-strap beard—shine a very particular light on what ADHD does to make our lives so tough. And so special.

We're gonna have fun. We're gonna have some laughs. We might even cry. I promise you I've cried many times while writing this book, although mainly at the editor's notes. She's kind of a bully.

---

[1] That and I had no idea how hard it would be to get my dog, Yuma, off Tibetan yak shank after she got a taste for it. Daddy's gotta earn, bitch!

Foreword

Did you know that you can't just draw a big dick on a page and call it Chapter 5? (Even after having the Chapter 4 skin removed!) I thought it would be a nice palate cleanser and help the neurofabulous reader feel good about getting through a whole chapter in one go but nooooooo, it's all, "Darcy, that's inappropriate!" Like, hello? Have you seen my brand? I'm just trying to give the dear reader what they came for: a giant serving of a big ol' D!

But alas, here I am putting that big ol' D into dysfunction.

Shit, right? That's what this is about. Because can I be honest? Even though you're reading all these words and sentences on the same page at the same time, that's not how I wrote them. In true ADHD style, it all came in fits and starts, and the starting was the hardest part—which, believe me, kicks the shit out of you when it comes to writing a foreword.

That inability to get started on a task, or a big project, comes from a particular place for those of us who have ADHD, and that cluster of symptoms is called executive dysfunction. Now, because of its name, executive dysfunction is often confused with the phenomenon of being lewdly harassed by impotent old men from corporate. So okay, let's start with the clinical definition because that's easy—I can google it, copy, and paste it here:

Easy as that.

Fuck, I forgot to paste it.

Here:

Executive dysfunction is a term used to describe faults or weaknesses in the cognitive process that organizes thoughts and activities, prioritizes tasks, manages time efficiently, and makes decisions.

Oh shit, now my font is different. Google, you're not helping with the imposter syndrome here!

Okay, I left my office briefly to get my husband to show me how to change the font back.[2] But then I also had a slice of gluten-free toast and watered my plants. This is not going to be easy for either of us. Ooh, speaking of water, drink some (a famously neglected task for us neurofabulous warriors)! And take your meds; we're in this for a long haul together.

But one important thing did happen on my tea-toast-and-tenderness break, however. While I was tea-bagging my Euro-Disney mug and quietly laughing in French, I looked down at the beautiful bamboo and élastique onesie I was wearing (I know that's technically the past tense but I'm still wearing it, I'm not typing naked—I hardly do that even half the time) and had a revelation. (Bear with me, I swear it's relevant.)

When people see the gentle folds of my flowing, floral apparel, they tend to think two things:

"That reminds me of the Georgia O'Keeffe print I saw in that lesbian's garage."

"That is a beautiful muumuu."

When people compliment me on my "muumuus," I smile and thank them on the outside because there's no point going full diva and some folks are allergic to cats.[3] But technically, I don't wear muumuus, I wear playsuits. These distinctions are important. And if you're wondering what the difference is, first, maybe you should have bought a book about leisurewear because it sounds like you

---

2 To make reading easier for ADHD individuals, this book uses a sans serif font. Don't say I never did anything for you.

3 Last word to be read with theatrical flourish, obviously.

have a lot of brushing up to do; and second, it's very simple: a playsuit is like a muumuu with legs.

A muumuu. With legs.

The idea is like a good edible: you don't even really notice it at first and then suddenly it just knocks you on your ass. A muumuu with legs is not only a wonderful thing on its own, but also the perfect metaphor for life. Be comfortable, but be practical. Be chill, but challenge yourself. Luxuriate, but struggle in bathrooms.

Then I realized that my book could be a muumuu with legs. Comfortable. Adaptive. Something you hold in your hands while you sit on the toilet.

So here's my promise to you: I've written this thing so that whether you're a little neurofabulous minx cracking your first book since fake-crying to fit in with the rest of the class during *Charlotte's Web* or a neuromayonnaise speed-reader who goes through this season's award winners before they go into paperback, you'll feel welcome in these pages. If you're a part of the neurotypical majority, then guess what: this book works as a regular, cover-to-cover venture for you to plod through at your leisure.

But if—like the insomniac with the bondage kink—you tend to struggle between the covers, this bad bitch has also been built to your specifications. You don't have to read it in the order it's been printed. We've left you an alternative trail of breadcrumbs to follow, which is particularly fucking generous of me because I'm celiac. THE THINGS I DO FOR YOU CREEPS! At the end of every chapter, you'll be given the chance to CHOOSE YOUR OWN DISTRACTION and follow the path through the book that makes the most sense to you. That option begins at the end of the next bit, which is the introduction. Obviously, you have to read the foreword and the introduction first; we're not animals. But after that, you do you.

And we're going to get you through this book, chapter by chapter, page by page, sentence by sentence, word by word, letter by letter. How do I know you're going to be able to read this book that way? In your way? Because I have ADHD. And that's how I wrote it.

Let me close now by telling you DO NOT READ THIS BOOK.

See, that's how I trick myself into doing things because of my ED. (Again, executive dysfunction NOT erectile dysfunction—another reason for my original Chapter 5 idea.)

So we're not going to read this book and we're not going to have fun doing it.

Good talk.

Enjoy not reading this book as much as I enjoyed not writing it.

AN IMAGINED LITERARY CALL

Phone rings

Male voice: Hello?

Darcy: Hi, is this Mr. Fitzhugh?

Male voice: Yes, this is he.

Darcy: You may not remember me, Mr. Fitzhugh, but you taught me high school English many years ago. My name is Darcy Michael.

Fitzhugh: Oh my God!

Darcy: Oh, wow—it's always humbling and surprising to find out just how popular my videos are, even with—

Fitzhugh: Videos?

Darcy: Yeah, my videos ... online? Why did you say, "Oh my God"?

Fitzhugh: I'd just assumed that after Trudeau legalized marijuana you would have long since drowned in some sort of bong water accident.

Darcy: No, I'm still here.

Fitzhugh: And just how did you get this number may I ask?

Darcy: Oh, um ... well, I'm not proud of this, but ... do you remember getting a series of late-night phone calls in the spring of 1997?

Fitzhugh: Well, there was a spate of crank calls in that period from some primordial, low-giggling miscreant who thought nothing was funnier than to announce various broadly phallic items which my body might accommodate. "Hey, I bet a zucchini fits you! I bet a Canada Goose fits you!" The caller's puerile delight suggested that they had never before considered the homophone in any capacity.

Darcy: Well, speaking of homo phone ...

Fitzhugh: The calls introduced a nearly unbearable tension into my marriage, as my then-wife assumed that the furtive ringing followed by rapid hang-ups must be coming from an illicit partner. I came to learn that this was a paranoid projection on her part, as she had for many months been liaising with the man who had redone our kitchen cabinetry in the North Burnaby home he shared with three generations of his Italian-Canadian family. Why do you ask about the phone calls?

Darcy: Oh, uh ... because that person probably got the number from the same place as me. Anyway, I'm calling to share some news.

Fitzhugh: If this is about Neil Ferryweather's receipt of the Greater Sudbury Regional Award for Poetic Achievement or Smelting, I am, of course, already well aware.

Darcy: No! I'm calling because I don't know if you remember, but you weren't always very encouraging to me as an English student.

Fitzhugh: As I recall, you once asked me if a semicolon was the same thing as a small intestine.

Darcy: Well, I'm calling to tell you that despite you not believing in me, I just got a deal to write a book! A book with a fancy New York publisher! So how do you like them apples?

Fitzhugh: Those apples.

Darcy: Would you fucking—I never thought I'd be saying this to somebody else, but can you just stick to the topic at hand please?!

Fitzhugh: What could you possibly be equipped to write a book about, Darcy?

Darcy: Well, as it happens, way back in the nineties, when I was still a high school student, there was something about me that you didn't know.

Fitzhugh: Oh, believe me, we knew. I thought you were going to stare a hole into the crotch of Kevin L.'s sweatpants. That's why I moved the desks!

Darcy: Not that! I had ADHD. Totally unmanaged, totally unmedicated, undiagnosed right into my early middle age.

Fitzhugh: Interesting.

Darcy: And when they first told me I was going to write a book about it, the only thing I could think was, "I can't." I thought of all the red ink on those assignments I handed in to you, the trouble I had keeping up with my reading ... I thought of the shaky way I tried to fake my way through those classes and wondered if I was just going to fake my way through this, too.

Fitzhugh: That ... sounds very trying.

Darcy: But then it struck me all at once—over the past few years, while I've been learning about my diagnosis and the best ways forward for me and my husband, I've connected with millions of people around the world. Something about the way we've been trying to figure things out has struck a chord with people. They can relate. They can see themselves in my journey, they can laugh along with me, and when I forgive myself, they can forgive themselves. And that's why I can write a book. That's why I need to.

Fitzhugh: I see. Darcy, I'd like to thank you for calling. This has been a humbling experience for me. For all these years, I'd just assumed that you were stoned in class—

Darcy: Oh, to be clear I was also high as fuck, on the daily.

Fitzhugh: Now, to be clear, as you're aware, I'm a male baby boomer whom you just called on the landline I still have from the 1990s, so I don't really believe in ADHD.

Darcy: [pounds telephone against forehead]

Fitzhugh: Nevertheless, from a pedagogical perspective, I see this as a story of redemption. Perhaps ... perhaps for both of us. And I hope that when you finish your book, which I now believe that you can do, I hope that you will send me a copy.

Darcy: Thank you, Mr. Fitzhugh. It's a deal. I'll send you a signed, hardcover copy from the first batch off the printing press. And sir, when it arrives?

Fitzhugh: Yes, Darcy?

Darcy: I HOPE IT FITS YOOOUUUUUUUU!!!!!!!

IMPORTANT TERMS

These are the terms, phrases, and mildly chaotic concepts that come up a lot in this book. And, frankly, in my brain. Consider this your ADHD survival guide slash decoder ring. Skim it, memorize it, ignore it, and come back later when you're confused. No rules. Just vibes. And definitions.

Body Doubling

- Darcy's definition: A way to get stuff done by tricking your brain into thinking it's a team project. Like an orgy but more productive and less sticky.

- "Formal" definition: A productivity strategy based around having someone nearby (physically or virtually) to help an ADHD brain focus and complete tasks. An accountability buddy-system.

Burnout

- Darcy's definition: When your brain files for emotional bankruptcy so your body joins in (and alternatively, what my father thinks of me).

- "Formal" definition: A state of physical, emotional, and mental exhaustion caused by prolonged stress—often from masking, overcommitting, and/or untreated ADHD.

Choice Paralysis

- Darcy's definition: Staring at forty-seven kinds of toothpaste on the shelf and leaving the store with gum and existential dread instead.

- "Formal" definition: Difficulty making decisions due to overwhelming options or fear of making the "wrong" choice, often tied to ADHD-related executive dysfunction.

Dopamine-Digging

- Darcy's definition: That thing where you suddenly need to reorganize your spice rack at 2 a.m. to feel alive again.

- "Formal" definition: The ADHD brain's constant hunt for dopamine, leading to impulsive or novel-seeking behaviors to stimulate focus and/or joy.

Executive Function

- Darcy's definition: The mental CEO who called in sick years ago and never came back.

- "Formal" definition: A set of cognitive skills (like planning, organizing, and prioritizing) that help us manage tasks—often impaired in the ADHD brain.

Hyperfixation

- Darcy's definition: It's not "just a hobby"—it's my whole identity until further notice. Now let me show you my LEGO collection before I get bored with it.

- "Formal" definition: An intense and prolonged focus on a specific interest or task, common in ADHD brains, often to the exclusion of everything else (including food and sleep).

Iceberg Theory

- Darcy's definition: Only 10 percent of the mess is showing—the other 90 percent is a panic party under the surface. And no, those bubbles aren't from the bathtub jets; I had gluten.

- "Formal" definition: The idea that what people see externally is only a small portion of what's actually going on inside, especially with neurodivergent experiences.

Imposter Syndrome

- Darcy's definition: Despite doing great things, you're still convinced you're one wrong email away from being exposed as a fraud. Or in my case, being an "author."

- "Formal" definition: A psychological pattern where individuals doubt their abilities and fear being "found out" as incompetent, despite evidence of success.

Impulse Control

- Darcy's definition: The tiny bouncer in your brain who's supposed to say "maybe don't"—but he's on a smoke break.

- "Formal" definition: The ability to pause before reacting or making decisions; often weakened in the ADHD brain due to issues with executive functioning.

Love-Bombing

- Darcy's definition: Not to be confused with Russia's treatment of Ukraine, love bombing is the emotional version of binge-watching someone you just met.

- "Formal" definition: A behavioral pattern where someone overwhelms another with attention and affection, often as a way to control or fast-track intimacy.

Masking

- Darcy's definition: Acting "normal" so you don't get weird looks—or get fired.

- "Formal" definition: The act of camouflaging ADHD symptoms to fit into social or professional norms, which can be exhausting and unsustainable.

Mirroring

- Darcy's definition: Becoming a human chameleon so people "like" you—only to forget who you are by bedtime. Am I a hockey player or did I just go to a pub for the playoffs? Either way, I'm in bed with a jockstrap.

- "Formal" definition: Imitating others' behaviors, speech, or interests (often unconsciously) as a way to connect or fit in, especially in social settings.

Object Permanence

- Darcy's definition: If I can't see it, it's dead to me. Which is why I just stopped opening my credit card statement.

- "Formal" definition: The ability to understand that objects and people still exist even when not visible; ADHD brains often forget this, hence the abandoned laundry in the washer since Tuesday.

Rejection Sensitive Dysmorphia (RSD)

- Darcy's definition: When someone says, "I can't hang out" and your brain screams, "I knew it, they hate me and I should move to the woods."

- "Formal" definition: An intense emotional reaction to perceived rejection or criticism, common in people with ADHD.

Sensory Overload

- Darcy's definition: When your shirt's tag, the hum of the fridge, and someone breathing near you all file noise complaints at once and it's time for your bones to jump out of your skin.

- "Formal" definition: An overwhelming response to sensory input—sound, light, touch, etc.—due to heightened sensitivity in many neurodivergent people.

Time Blindness

- Darcy's definition: When five minutes can last an hour or disappear completely—there is no time, only vibes. And the vibes are late.

- "Formal" definition: Difficulty perceiving the passage of time accurately, which can lead to chronic lateness, underestimating tasks, or surprise all-nighters.

INTRODUCTION
HOW LONG HAVE YOU HAD ADHD?
OR WHERE DO I GET OFF WRITING A BOOK?

Picture it—Sicily, 1935.

Sorry, I've been watching a lot of *Golden Girls*.

Alright listen, I have to admit this is not like me. With ADHD, getting started is not usually the problem. The middle? Sure, she's always a spiky little fucker. *Finishing?* Almost impossible. Don't look now, but about a hundred pages from the end of this thing I cop out and declare that rest of it is just a "mindfulness sketchbook." (The publisher has asked me to tell you to please strike this last sentence from the record until you have purchased the book; also, they told me to say that reading this paragraph in an airport bookstore while waiting for your flight is a form of "intellectual shoplifting.") But getting started? Hell, getting things started is my jam! If I stuck with everything I started, you might know me instead for my hanging-plant art, my knitting, or my home drywalling. That's assuming you do know me from my standup comedy, the live shows I do around the world with my husband, Jer, or the funny little videos we make about our neurodivergent home life for tens of millions of online viewers. Hell, maybe you don't know me from any of that. Maybe you're reading these words at an estate sale, in which case I can only say, *"Shame on you! Death is no time to look for a deal! Go buy your own copy and bury the departed with this one, as they would have wanted."*

The truth is, I have no idea how to start a book. But I always love a good mysterious hook off the top, something with a little bit of mystique, elegance, and an exotic locale. And you know I'm a whore for building the brand, so ideally there'll be a throbbing current of neurodiversity pulsating its way through the text like a middle-aged guy who can't catch his breath but won't stop pumping his fists as he snakes his way across the dance floor.

So okay. Let's start the story here:

Los Angeles, California; a six-bedroom almost-mansion in the Hollywood Hills.

The year was 2018, just shortly after my thirty-eighth birthday. (Okay, that may or may not be where I got the image of the guy pumping his fists across the dance floor.) I was perched high atop this dreamy Tinseltown vista with my writing partner at the time and two television producers. It's hard to imagine a 1:1 writer-to-producer ratio in these days of AI-generated IP crossover content, but this was way back in the prehistoric days of the iPhone XS. You don't even remember that one, do you? No, no, don't look it up on your phone! Stay with me, in the moment! First of all: ugh, irony. Secondly: this book is supposed to help both of us concentrate.

So let's get back to the Hollywood Hills. We were there to write *Darcy*—a sitcom about my life commissioned by Canada's leading broadcaster, CTV.

Let me just take a second here. You're doing great and I don't want us to get distracted from the main plotline. But I do think I should take a minute to address what people have always said about my work: *"Darcy, your titles are so creative! How do you come up with names like* Darcy *for a sitcom about your life, and 'Darcy & Jer' for your channel with your husband, Jer?"* Fuck. I literally didn't realize people were being sarcastic until I just typed it out. So far being an author is the shits.

I had never felt more alive than I had in the days leading up to that LA trip—a trip that meant realizing a dream I'd dreamt since I was seven years old and I first saw an episode of *Roseanne*. (Listen, back off, I didn't know, okay? Roseanne didn't have Twitter yet).

On this particular day, the four of us were sitting around this gorgeous kitchen island, making bacon and eggs, cracking jokes, and celebrating an exciting new adventure. All this while staying in a house I couldn't afford to even look at on Zillow let alone be living in for a whole week. The bacon sizzled and crackled, waiting to be flipped in the pan. (Okay, I'm sorry to draw attention to it but that's the first literary device so far in the book, and honey, I nailed that bitch. I was too stoned to remember anything from high school English except literary devices because I remember thinking how bong water sounded like somebody giggling, and from that moment on, how could I ever forget analogies or figurative language! Anyway, in this case, the bacon sizzling and crackling as it waits symbolizes the hopeful expectancy and excitement in the room as we wait for one more person to arrive. The anticipation is real. Also, the bacon symbolizes breakfast.)

The doorbell rang and then the door opened ... this entrance, I will learn, is very on point. First entered Maple, who was a golden doodle. I was instantly in love. She was calm, she was friendly, she was my new best friend. Behind Maple, in walked our showrunner—the person we'd hired to be in charge of shaping *Darcy*; little did I know, he wasn't going to leave the real-life, italics-free Darcy as he found him, either. (I mean that in a foreshadowy way, not a sexy way.) For you peons unfamiliar with the inner workings of the biz we call show, a showrunner is the person who oversees the entire creation, direction, and production of a show. They run it, if you will. It's an incredibly vital and important job, and to do it, we had hired someone I'd looked up to for years: Bruce McCulloch. Yeah, that's right; basically, a human golden doodle.

One of the founding members of The Kids in the Hall, the writer and director of Molly Shannon's *Superstar*, director of multiple episodes of *Schitt's Creek*, and so many more credits that if I keep listing them his ego will continue to inflate beyond the capacities of his delicate Canadian infrastructure so I'll leave it at this: he's a comedy icon, and he'd chosen to work with us fools on a silly little sitcom.

At this point, I was unusually nervous, my palms sweaty, my knees weak, my arms heavy … oh God, Siri, stop dictating everything you hear!

Sorry, I turned the music off.

We're back.

Bruce looked at me and said,

"Good morning, son, are you ready to change the world?"

Bruce has a kind soul and a disarming smile, but there is also a devilish glint in his eyes that just says, "Let's be mischievous together …"

We all sat down to begin working, because that's what we were there to do. And I was a grown-up show-businessman who'd been entrusted with a sitcom named after me by a leading Canadian broadcaster, so I was ready to dig in and work, WOO. B-U-S-Y—not now! No time!

We started by pulling up the original script my writing partner and I had put together months before. We'd worked on it relentlessly, in the hopes that Bruce would come along and add some jokes here and there and that then we'd be locked in and ready to film.

We weren't quite ready for his notes, which were ... copious and detailed.

But in fact, I wasn't quite ready for anything just yet. I needed a quick coffee and, back in those days, a cigarette. (For you youngsters, imagine basically a disposable paper vape.) So we all headed out to the patio overlooking Los Angeles for a less-toxically-masculine *Entourage* tableau moment while Maple went for a pee. I smoked while playing in the Airbnb's yard. (Just one more quick aside, and this'll be the last one in the book, I promise: the problem with Airbnbs is that no one is ever living there long enough to actually take care of the yard!) So here was this beautiful aloe plant about the height of my upper thigh, just massive but covered in leaves from a dying evergreen. So now there I was pushing the leaves off and trying to figure out why this evergreen was sick.

"Okay, son, let's head inside ..." Bruce always called me son, right from the very beginning. I don't think I would have let anyone else call me that in a working environment, but somehow, from him, it just made me feel nice. So I let it slide.

We headed inside but, before getting back to work—well not technically back to work but you know what I mean—I was just going to just send a quick message on Airbnb to the owners to let them know that they should have an arborist come by to look at that evergreen tree, because I'd hate for it to die and fall into their infinity pool. Not to mention that the aloe plant deserves a bit more respect. *"Hey, did you all realize that 'arborist' is practically an anagram for Airbnb except for that they have some different letters ... yes, it was just a cigarette."*

"Okay, let's open the script ..." said Bruce.

"Yeah!" Oh, but as we do, I wanted to make sure that he would catch the subtle but important reference to *Roseanne* that I had thrown in the opening scene, so I just pulled up the episode on my computer really quickly to show him.

Bruce reached over, closed my laptop, and gave me a very fatherly look. And suddenly I realized, *"Oh ... this is why he called me son. Okay, Dad, sorry, let's get to work."*

It was coming up on an hour since he'd arrived, and sure, we'd done nothing, but for me it was helping to break the tension and nervous energy I had that day. But then Bruce raised his face to me, a question waiting in his brown eyes and in the twitch of his Mona Lisa smile.

On *The Kids in the Hall*, arguably the greatest sketch comedy show ever created except that Canadians don't really like to argue, Bruce was famous for playing characters who combined brash effrontery with delicate vulnerability: Gavin "Cabbage Head" Brucio. I'm writing all this now because at that moment, across that table, with his question loaded and ready, Bruce's face had that same combination of features. To this day, I'm still not totally sure if he asked me this in the spirit of teasing discipline, as a showrunner trying to whip his writers' room into disciplinary shape, or whether he did it to save my life.

But Bruce McCulloch asked me, *"How long have you had ADHD?"*

ADHD?! What the fuck does he mean? My mind raced immediately back to elementary school, where one kid in my class was diagnosed with ADHD and, as the teacher was trying to explain to the rest of the class that we would just have to ignore him, he was standing on his desk pouring glue down his pants.[1]

I'm not standing on a desk!

I don't have glue anywhere near me! My crotch is *barely* sticky!

ADHD?! *You're* the one who had a cabbage for a head, asshole!

I had turned thirty-eight years old four days before we arrived in LA. Thirty-eight years. Thirty-eight years and no one had ever said a word to me about ADHD, and now one of my idols was sitting across from me with his fucking mischievous little elfin grin on his face, this glint of all-knowing in his eyes, and a look that said "I can see right through you shithead, so sit down and get to work. *I AM BRUCIO!"*

Maple came over and laid across my lap like a weighted blanket and we all got to work (except her—lazy bitch just slept), but the entire time my brain was elsewhere wondering who the fuck did this guy think he is? Coming into my (rented by someone else) mansion to work on my TV show and after an hour he disrespects me like this?!

A rage was swelling inside me. In my mind's eye, I could see myself throwing Maple off my lap and diving across the table to grab his chiffon scarf and using it to throw the little man around the room like a tetherball. (We'll address ADHD rage in a later chapter, FYI ... so for now GET OFF MY BACK!)

But another part of me was asking ... what if Bruce McCulloch wasn't being an asshole? What if he hadn't come into my mansion and disrespected me?[2] I mean, in theory, we had picked him as

---

1   Virtually impossible to ignore—true story.

2   Not my mansion.

Introduction

showrunner because of his vision and insight, right? (Plus, a willingness to work for Canadian dollars.)

What if he was just ... right?

WHAT DOES THIS MEAN FOR YOU?

Well, in some ways, it'll take the rest of this book to answer that question. In another way, it'll take the rest of my life to answer that question. (I mean that in a very spiritual, philosophical sense, but also: smash that follow/subscribe button—mama's microsuede loafers ain't gonna bejewel themselves!) For now, try to keep these things in that fast-moving mind:

- Finding out you have ADHD for the first time as an adult is complicated. For some people it comes as a relief—now that you've named it you can do something about it. BUT it may also come with deep resentment that it took this long to begin the journey.

- It's important to acknowledge when you're feeling out of your depth. Imposter syndrome is real (ironically, I actually feel qualified saying that) and it's totally common for people who struggle with processing their thoughts and emotions. But you got yourself here and you deserve to be here.

- ADHD can be incredibly isolating. Getting stuck in your own head and keeping the inner saboteur/shithead from taking the lead is a constant battle. In those moments, pet the puppy (or do whatever your comfort equivalent is) and try to focus on listening outward rather than inward.

CHOOSE YOUR OWN DISTRACTION

→ If you want to know how I came to get my own sitcom, turn to page 141.

→ If you want to hear the story of my first time getting life advice from a Kids in the Hall guy, turn to page 131.

→ To get an idea of how I went thirty-eight years without a single person suggesting I had ADHD, keep reading ...

1.
WHERE DOES ADHD COME FROM?
PORTRAIT OF THE ARTIST AS A YOUNG NEURODIVERGENT

Nobody knows exactly where ADHD comes from. I like quoting from the "Causes" section on the UK's National Health Services website,[1] because then I get to imagine it in a fun English accent and that helps me pay attention. Those lovely Brits lay the likely blame/credit for ADHD at the feet of genetics as well as brain function and structure (the old "junction and Luxor" in Cockney rhyming slang). They also outline certain groups at risk—hey, if I know the English, that's probably the Irish, am I right?!—including babies born before the thirty-seventh week of pregnancy. (Which is, tragically, often the very last time in their lives that people with ADHD show up early for anything.)

As with any complex issue with multiple, overlapping, and uncertain causes affecting the most intimate details of real people's precious and challenging lives, a lot of people on the internet and in your extended family know exactly everything about ADHD:

---

1   https://www.nhs.uk/conditions/adhd-adults/ (Go see what a non-porny website looks like for once, ya creeps!)

1. It's a made-up disease for lazy people to hide behind now that luxury steamship travel has been phased out!
2. It comes from marshmallows in breakfast cereal!
3. Stoners are doing too much pot, and thus, ADHD!
4. It's a phase, like homosexuality or whooping cough!
5. Baby mobiles are too intricate nowadays!
6. It's a scam for undergraduates to get extra time writing their Wokeness exams!
7. It comes from the lack of marshmallows in breakfast cereal!
8. Stoners are doing too much pot, and thus, ADHD!
9. Kids' cartoons are edited too quickly! When I was a kid, you got to watch the same Flintstones background image cycle for eleven minutes straight, which taught you how to concentrate!
10. Stoners are doing too much pot, and thus, ADHD!

What sucks about all this dumbassery is that we can't just swat it away like we can the ignorant theories about, for instance, why I'm gay, because I don't have a solid answer to give. Obviously, I'm gay because my mom let me drink a pink can of Crush cream soda at a family reunion when I was seven—but why do I have ADHD?

For that matter, how did I make it so long without anybody noticing? I was thirty-eight years old when Bruce McCulloch diagnosed me, which I'll remind you, when you're gay and married is basically like mid-fifties.

Also, my editor and the publishers have asked me to stress for you that sketch comedy legend Bruce McCulloch is not the sole source of my ADHD diagnosis. Obviously, after he raised the possibility, I went straight to an actual authority who knows about this kind of stuff and can make these kinds of assessments—but when I asked Joe Rogan, he said I had it, too! Okay, I didn't go see Rogan about it; I hate to ruin our cold plunges with a lot of talk.[2] Instead, I went to see a specialist and got a legitimate diagnosis from a trained medical professional. But how did I make it almost forty years without anybody noticing?

I was born into show business when my mom Cheryl's water broke in a movie theater on April 1, 1980, technically the day before my birthday. She told me later that she kept her legs crossed until after midnight because there was no way she was giving birth to a fool, and ever since that day, like a Greek tragedy, my life has been proving to her that you can't escape your fate. (Well, like a Greek tragedy but somehow ... gayer?) Meanwhile, my dad, Tom, who in those days was still on the Toronto SWAT team—I know! You didn't know I was half butch, did ya?—showed up to the maternity ward two days late because he was on a double shift somewhere and fell asleep. As he walked into the hospital, all Dad could hear was one baby screaming bloody murder and he thought: "Well, fuck—I bet that one's mine." Tom was SWAT but he coulda been a detective.

I don't really have any memories of the first eight years of my life, which I used to think was normal, but looking back now I'm thinking it might be further evidence that my mind was already spinning off the walls even back then. If a regular brain is Velcro, think of mine as one of those sleek marble accent walls that really fucking pops but that you can't stick anything to.

So, what happened in 1988 that got the memory train chuggin'? Our family moved across the country from Pickering, Ontario, to Lynn Valley, on Vancouver's North Shore, when Dad traded in his SWAT status for a slower, safer, killing-me-inside-compromise-for-my-family corporate security job. We drove across the country

---

2   My lawyers/the cricket who acts as my external conscience have advised me to point out that this is a joke and that I have never had any Joe Rogan experiences.

in Mom's Volvo (that's VOLVO for you Freudian creeps looking for an alternative to the pink Crush theory), and for reasons I can't explain, eight-year-old Darcy felt immediately at home as soon as we entered British Columbia. Honestly, my conscious memory flips on like the color when Dorothy enters Oz the second our car hit the Rockies. I had never seen anything so beautiful in my whole little life. People who didn't live through the eighties have no idea just how big the Rockies were back then—and Rocky IV was filmed in my new home, Vancouver!

As the old saying goes, you can take the man out of the SWAT team, but without quality mental health care and a culture of openness and support, you can't take the post-traumatic stress out of the ex-SWAT man. Every night at dinner, it became my unofficial duty to somehow make Dad laugh in order to set the tone for the evening. One night I'll never forget, when I was eleven, I watched him from the living room window as he got out of the car with a box of Tim Horton's donuts in his arms. With his hands full, he struggled to get the front door unlocked and, in a fit of rage, threw the box of donuts across the lawn.

It pained me to see that. Those were my donuts. From that evening onward, like a dog with an unmatched internal clock, I always made sure to greet my dad at the open door when he got home. Life can be cruel, but it can't be cruller-less.

All of this was around the time when, in theory, somebody should have been noticing that I had ADHD. The elementary school years are when many neurodivergent little boys are identified, even while many of their female peers remain overlooked. (Well luckily, that's the last time THAT happens, right ladies?!) Oh, we laugh to cover the tears. A medical article called "Miss. Diagnosis: A Systematic Review of ADHD in Adult Women," which yes, I may have only chosen because it had the best title, says that even though adult ADHD diagnoses are 1:1 male-to-female, the boy-to-girl numbers are 3:1. But I wasn't identified as having ADHD. I was identified as short, fat, loud, lippy, and obnoxious (and while we didn't really have this language back then, that was also how I self-identified). Which is not to say that reality and I saw eye to eye on everything. Like with all kids, there was a gap between the way life was unfolding in the real world and the way things were going in my head. For instance, when I sang George Michael's "I Want Your Sex" to a group of boys in the locker room, they all thought it was hilarious.

"That's interesting," I thought. "I was pretty sure it was a triumph of Marlene Dietrich–style seductive cabaret charisma, but yeah, okay, I guess I'll take hilarious."

And in fairness, I probably didn't hit all the ADHD student markers. Like in Band, you'd probably figure the ADHD kid would stereotypically play something dynamic, like the drums, or something flighty, like a piccolo flute. And what did I play? I played the baritone. And now you're thinking, "The baritone what, Darcy? Baritone saxophone? Baritone guitar?" Nope, what I played is literally called a baritone instrument. That's how fucking lame it is. No one's ever heard of it. I wasn't quite fat enough to carry a tuba, so they made me play the baritone horn.

One of the countless advantages of a piccolo flute over a baritone horn besides easy ADHD identification is ease of transportation. If they want, a kid can tuck a piccolo flute behind their ear like an architect with a pencil. And the baritone instrument, you ask? Why, for lugging around the baritone, if you're lucky, your dad will build you a rolling luggage rack–style cart with bungee cords for pulling your instrument securely around. One time, I couldn't find the bungee cords, because Dad had needed them to hold the car trunk closed. So to make up for the absence, he had given me some rope and Scotch tape.

And fuck it, maybe that's how I got through school without a diagnosis or meds. With rope, some Scotch tape, and a prayer.

Anyone who's made it into adulthood before getting diagnosed with ADHD knows the way life can become a series of complex, sometimes beautiful workarounds. Beautiful, until they pile up so high they fall in on you.

Without any small flute or glue in my pants (how's that for the puberty talk?), nobody could tell I had ADHD. Instead, with two friends and two friends only (Jeff and Chris; good dudes), with angelic cherub cheeks and a John Candy hero-worship complex, I was slotted into a different school category: Theater Kid. I know—Jer was as surprised as you are to hear that I used to have a flair for the dramatic! (You obviously can't see this, but I just threw the cape I was wearing down from my lower ear across my chest in a big sweeping motion and knocked half of a mango and chia seed oat milk smoothie onto the floor. Yuma keeps looking up at me with this weird mix of gratitude and contempt.)

So from the school's perspective, I wasn't acting out—I was *acting*! And in terms of "labels for Darcy Michael" that the school administrators were quietly hoping his parents would hip to without having to be officially alerted, "hyperactive" ranked way lower than "blossoming homosexual." (When the time came for prom, the school refused to allow me just to bring my boyfriend as my date. They insisted instead that we had to be accompanied by one of our girl friends. I didn't have the heart to point out that in their opposition to innocent gay teen monogamy they had not only proposed but were demanding a polyamorous ambisexual adolescent throuple.)

The truth is, there are a million and a half ways that those of us with ADHD learn to cope with and mask our symptoms, even if doing it is slowly killing us inside. Or quickly killing us, inside and out. One study, headed by University of Toronto Professor Esme Fuller-Thomson, discovered that fully half of adults with ADHD had experienced a substance abuse problem. I find that statistic completely overwhelming—not least because I don't know whether it's optimistic or pessimistic to point out that it means half of adults with ADHD haven't had a substance abuse problem. (Oh, who are we kidding; we all know the half that didn't just forgot to finish filling out the survey.)

I'm being funny, because this is a funny book. That's sort of the deal. But this part isn't a million laughs because the things people will do to hide or to deal with ADHD that they don't yet know about or understand can be extremely painful.

Sometimes it's playing up a totally false and hurtful reputation as a flake, or a klutz, or an airhead, to cover frequent lapses in memory or follow-through. Sometimes it's abandoning, or just never even starting, professional or academic opportunities that you know you just can't handle, even if you can't understand why. For me, as a little boy, the need to beat back the chaos in my brain led to me keeping a room so ordered and tidy that my parents were genuinely worried that I had OCD. (Or worse, a gay interior decorator. Well, I've got good news, and I've got bad news ...)

So the sooner you can get your official diagnosis, the sooner you can get real help and guidance. There are also questionnaires online compiled by doctors and scientists to help with assessment. These valuable tools look absolutely nothing like this:

Darcy Michael's Entirely Unscientific ADHD Questionnaire

1. Before starting this, did you google to see whether anyone had ever done a kids' show about a group of intrepid little philosophers called The Questioneers?
2. Which of the following best describes you: i) always on the go; b) probably have ADHD; 3) [returns to reread question].
3. Do you have trouble coping even with kind and good-faith criticism or rejection?

4. Did you think that last question was directed particularly at you?
5. Are you still taking this test?
6. What day is it? (Trust me, this stupid fucking question comes up a LOT.)
7. Do you often experience big shifts in mood? Don't you think they can be great?!
8. Isn't it all just too fucking much sometimes?
9. How many twos were there in the last year you did your taxes?
10. Do you have issues with impulse control—be honest, did you just take off your clothes?
11. DO YOU FIND LOUD NOISES DISTURBING?
12. True or False: You have Choice Paralysis.
13. Do you sometimes have trouble remembering the particular word for a given ... ah ... shit, you know what I mean, like the right word for that specific—you know when a thing is happening? Not "Asian," but it's in that neighborhood. I think it starts with a "T"? Oh my God, I know this! The Italian guy, with the abs ... Situation! Situation. Sorry, it doesn't start with a "T," I don't know what that was.
14. Are you the partner who has at this point taken over finishing the quiz? That's okay. This is Jer typing now. (Literary eye roll.)

AN EXPERIMENT: ADHD AND READING

Now, depending on how that test went, maybe you just experienced what I did that day in Hollywood: you just found out straight from an immortal comedy legend that you have ADHD.[3] For neurofabulous people navigating a neurotypical ("neuromayonaise," if you will) world, basic everyday tasks and pleasures can be experienced in completely different ways. Now, somebody get Alanis on the phone because shit's about to get ironic: oddly enough to bring up in a book, one of the hardest day-to-day joys to get a handle on is reading.

For a lot of us, reading was a school year's boot camp obstacle course we struggled our best through until graduation, then we chucked our mortarboards and never looked back. Others among us have looming Jenga piles of books on the nightstand, each one with a bookmark about fifteen pages in.

I know we're having fun here so far, and I don't want to break the [counts quickly] fifth(?) wall here too much, but if you're living with ADHD and you're making your way through this book with me ... I don't just tolerate you, I'm proud of you. And you should be proud of you, too.

There's no one little secret to reading with ADHD. But there is one big secret: do whatever works for you! From the scientific experts to those living with ADHD themselves, the prevailing wisdom seems to be to find the thing that makes it click in your particular case. That could mean reading in little chunks, even though that sounds gross. It could mean using a highlighter or pencil, although I must warn you that will affect resale value. It could mean just finding the perfectly quiet spot or finding the right friend to sit next to you while you read (or underneath you; in this space we do

---

3   The lawyers want me to insist here that my test is not actually diagnostic but that I really am an immortal comedy legend.

not judge what goes on between consenting adults!) You could even read it out loud to yourself. I actually wrote this book by speaking out loud, so I'm fine with you reading it out loud, too! The people on the bus might mind, but honestly in this attention deficit economy, I could use the help with promoting the book, so I HIGHLY RECOMMEND THIS BOOK WRITTEN BY DARCY MICHAEL, IT'S VERY FUNNY AND INFORMATIVE.

Okay, here's your assignment for the next section. I'm going to tell you a story now. It involves several of the characters you met in the last chapter if you didn't skip it (no judgement!), and it's one of the most important stories in my life. In fact, you may want to grab a tissue because this bitch gets weepy. And all I want you to do with this story is ... get through it, by hook or by crook. (Because you already paid for the book! Fun little rhyme.) Take whatever time you need, use whatever strategies help. And I'll be here the whole time. Because I'm the narrator, obviously.

Here we go ...

In the long, seedy history of stand-up comedy, comedians have gotten into certain bad habits and lazy shortcuts for the sake of cheap laughs. How many of us have watched in horror as some hack on stage tells everybody about the wacky airplane ride he took to the show just because he couldn't be bothered to think up anything more creative?

Pathetic.

Although, what is the deal with airport security?

Specifically, I remember the first time I went through the full-body x-ray scanner, arms at right angles above my head, like a Village People fan with arthritis. The idea of full-body transparency was so intimidating to me! What would the security agents see? (Also, at what point in the GI tract do pot brownies legally cease to be drugs?)

What I imagined that the agents would somehow see on the screen—what I thought would finally be exposed—was what I always felt like I was anyway: some kind of queer Russian nesting doll ... a fat gay child inside a fat gay teenager inside a fat gay man.

Now, why would a grown man who makes a living being gay-married on stage and on the internet even think of his queerness as something to be x-rayed? Something to be discovered by butch, disapproving-but-sexy security agents?

Well, it may be hard to imagine in our much more affirming and accepting new era,[4] but when I was a lad, and we had to gay uphill both ways in snow right up to our nipple rings—being queer was a secret to be hidden at all costs. And when you finally did Come Out, without any sense of how that news was going to land, you braced for the worst.

Another bad habit that stand-up comedians tend to indulge in? We have a tendency to take real, even meaningful experiences from our own lives, and hammer them into comedy shape on stage. Then after performing the story hundreds of times, we let the comedy version swallow up what happened in real life ... even in our own memory. (Some of my fellow ADHDers will be familiar with this process from their own private lives; "rehearsing" stories and anecdotes in their heads so that they get them right in social interactions. This concept is called "masking." Hey, if it's good enough for the people on Jimmy Fallon ...)

For many years, I told the story of my coming out on stage. And this is how I told it:

---

[4] Offer may not be valid outside big cities, please see in store for details.

I came out to my parents like twenty years ago, right? And my dad was on the Toronto SWAT team, so he's like alpha male. And my mom taught Sunday School my whole life, so she's like "Yay, Jesus!" And I came home from a party one night, and I walked into the house, and my parents sat me down and they just asked me if I was gay. And I was terrified. Because I had just come from a party where we had done a fuck-ton of mushrooms. And now I'm in the living room with my cop dad, my Jesus mom, and a dragon. And I don't know if it was the drugs, or if it was just time, but I had the courage and I looked at them and I said, "Yes, I'm gay."

And everything my parents believed turned on a dime. They said, "You're our son. It doesn't matter. We love you." The dragon was a little more homophobic. But, like, that moment? I've never forgotten that moment. That was unconditional love. That was Parenting 101, alright? And for the last twenty years, because of that, I have made a conscious effort not to eat a banana in front of my mother. That is my gift to her. I gotta stop deep-throating cucumbers in front of Dad, though—he's getting pissed!

I think we can all agree that story is great, and hilarious, possibly a master class in comic storytelling—quite conceivably the first thing since Mark Twain to attain, in the English language, such soaring heights of picaresque energy within the bounds of such literary economy, and virtually unparalleled in terms of the deep-throating-garden-vegetables-in-front-of-dad genre. But of course, it's not actually how it all really went down.

So here's how it did.

It was November 28, 1998. Bill Clinton's semen had stained the hearts of a generation, and the total collapse of the world's entire computing systems was still thirteen months away.

I was at home in the early afternoon with my mom. My relationship with my mom has always been great. Picture Sally Field and Julia

Roberts in *Steel Magnolias*, only Julia's super fat, a dude, and hasn't been diagnosed with diabetes.[5]

I had mentioned to Mom that I was spending the night at Dave's house for a party. Dave was my "best friend," at the time. This is what we called it back then, at the cusp of the new millennium, but I think now we'd call it a "situationship"—the situation being that we were horny eighteen year olds who didn't really realize that we could just be boyfriends.

"You spend a lot of time with Dave," said Mom.

"I love him," I blurted out of nowhere, to the shock of 100 percent of the people in the room (me and my mother). This is my earliest memory of impulse control and my lack thereof. (My latest memory of impulse control is the sixteen dining chairs I just bought online because I couldn't decide until I sat on them all, but that's another story for when Jer isn't here to scold me.) Adolescence is a part of life with more than its fair share of accidental ejaculations, but this one was a doozy.

My mom has a poker face like no one else, but there was a twitch in her lip, and I clocked it before she pursed them together. She didn't say anything. She just walked over and turned the kettle on, which in fairness is the middle-aged white lady version of honking a maritime distress airhorn. I knew we were about to get into it.

Now, with the benefit of hindsight, my brother and sister had both known by then that I was gay, and I think they had probably even told my mom before this. Not in, like, a tattletale way—"Mom! Darcy's not sharing! And he likes dong!"—but to prepare her delicate heart. Yet despite that, I could see her processing some real pain. She was concerned. She made us tea and patted the chair beside her as she sat. This wasn't an invitation; this was a

---

5   Yet?

non-negotiable sit-down. Are you hurt that I'm gay, or do you want to have a tea party, lady?! Pick a lane!!!

I started to cry. I honestly don't remember much beyond blubbering, *"I think I'm gay,"* and we sat. She was stunned; scared even. That made me cry more—I was hurting her. I knew from friends who'd come out that part of the process was to have a bag packed beforehand, to be ready to leave. I wasn't prepared. I hadn't meant to come out. Now, as we were talking, in my head I was also making a packing list and wondering how long I would have to get out of the house.

This was the nineties so, naturally, the conversation quickly became about AIDS. At the time it was ingrained in all of us that if you were gay, you stood a pretty good chance of dying of AIDS. And now that's all my poor sweet mama was thinking about; losing her son to a disease that we still barely understood.

She said she didn't understand why I "had to be gay," but she said that she wanted to. We hugged and cried.

"Am I still allowed to go to Dave's tonight?"

"Yes."

And so, I packed my "overnight" bag with everything I could think of that I might need in my life. I didn't know if I would be allowed back.

Poor, quiet Dave opened the door to me, trying to stay calm and unemotional as I wailed about losing my family. Then he did what Dave always did.

"You wanna get fucked up on mushrooms?"

There was a reason I loved him.

As the shrooms started to take hold a few hours later, I began to feel unfamiliar sensations. (Obviously not drug-related, as those would not have been unfamiliar.) I began feeling calmer and even, almost, ecstatic about what my new world was going to be like. I could just be me now. The prospect was thrilling.

I always describe coming out as like watching someone unclench their fist for the first time in their life.[6] It's tingly and odd-feeling but it's still your hand, it just feels—freer? (Is freer a word? I don't know, I'm on mushrooms, fuck off.)

Then it rang.

My Motorola flip phone. Thankfully, it was a Saturday, so I had free minutes!

(You see in the nineties, yes, we had AIDS, but we had even shittier cell phone plans.) My parents had one phone rule: If We Call, You Answer. Not answering was not a choice. Dave and I both stared at the phone across the room ringing like it was the red phone in the White House, waiting for the nuclear codes. Or the red phone in Batman's den, that probably works too.

I could barely read the "answer" button.

"Hello?"

It was my father. *"Come home."*

"I'm at Dave's with friends."

"Right. Now!"

Click.

---

6   Is it risky to use a fist-based metaphor here? Sure. But I'm trusting my readers to be fucking grown-ups, you creeps!

The line went dead.

(He had not gone into a tunnel.)

He sounded different. I couldn't place it, but I knew I had to go home. Any high that I had felt from the drugs was gone. The adrenaline had kicked into overdrive, and I was now as sober as a judge on whatever day of the week it is that judges don't get all fucked up.

I didn't know what I was walking into. Was it a goodbye?

Was it a shit kicking?

I had no idea. But I remember thinking, "Fuck it, if those little moments of freedom I was feeling from unclenching my fist were even a hint of how life could be for me as an out person, let's take my hits and get it over with."

At the front of our house was a split-level entry, with a landing at the front door that had six stairs going down to the basement on the right, and six stairs going up to the kitchen on the left.

As I walked in and stood on the landing, I could smell ... Jack Daniels. My dad was drunk?! My dad was almost never drunk. In fact, I will now interrupt this story to insert a list of every date upon which I have ever seen my dad drunk in my entire life:

November 28, 1998

He stood looming, like a giant at the top of the stairs, towering over me on the landing where I now felt smaller than I had ever felt before.

"Why didn't you tell me?" he boomed.

"I didn't want you to hate me."

Then he was a blur, coming down the stairs at me.

I flinched in terror—this was it, the moment everything would change forever.

He threw his arms around me like the bear that he is and held me tighter than he'd ever held me in my life. *"I could never hate you ... You're my son, you are me."*

I collapsed into his arms. I had never felt anything like this. What was it? Years of pain, releasing. Years of fear—fear of him—releasing. I sobbed. We both did. We just stood there holding each other and crying.

Then the door my dad's embrace had pushed me up against started to move. I thought we were breaking it from the pressure of the greatest hug of my life but no, it was my older brother, Wes. He was trying to get inside, and as he came in it was obvious he was drunk, too.

"Lookin' a little gay, guys!"

(Astute readers have figured out by this point that Wes is obviously "the dragon.") The three of us proceeded up to the kitchen to make some pasta in strange, eerie silence for a bit, all of us sobering up from our respective intoxicants, and my brother still slightly perplexed about what exactly he had walked in on. Well good, someone else in this house can be confused for a bit because I'm sick of it at this point.

After Wes ate, and left, Dad held me by the back of my neck and looked me dead in the eye.

"You're my son. I may not always understand you, and you're gonna drive me fucking nuts forever. But you never have to worry about me hating you. I love you. And I'll learn to love whoever you choose to love."

Reader, we've had a lot of laughs over the course of this book. (Which reminds me: you've rated and reviewed, right? These film rights are not going to sell themselves!) But as I sit a quarter century on, typing these sentences, reliving these memories in my mind for the first time in a long while, I can't help but think about the enormity of that night for me. My parents taught me so many lessons in one single day—lessons that I would use as a parent myself years later.

I know this isn't actually a self-help book—please, I can't stress this enough, do not continue reading if you're looking for help.[7] However, one lesson I did learn that day, which I feel confident in passing along: It's not a parent's job to understand everything; it's a parent's job to show up. My parents showed up for me that night, and in doing so they gave me the greatest gift I ever could have been given—the gift of the freedom to be me.

I don't know where I would be today if it wasn't for that night. But I do know that the love I have with Jeremy and Grace wouldn't have the foundation it does if I didn't have my parents to thank.

A few days later, I was back at school in theater class. Like the numberless army of little gay teens who came before and after me, I found safety in drama class, under the care of a teacher who continues, to this day, to be a mentor: Lloyd Burritt. I told Mr. Burritt that I had come out to my parents, and his response was pure 1990s: after checking if I had remembered to feed my Tamagotchi and safely stowed away my Pogs, Lloyd asked me if I had somewhere to stay.

It's another example of how things were for so long: not, "Congratulations!" but, in so many words, "Are you safe?"

Well, I was safe.

---

7   I mean, in a pinch you could use it to kill a big spider.

The next day, my mom arrived home to find a pile of five or six books on the front porch. Each one was about understanding your queer child in one way or another. I never asked, but I always knew that Lloyd dropped them off—he knew a good parent doesn't have to understand, but a great parent will want to.

I had a wonderful drama teacher.

And I have great parents.

Okay honestly, how fucking fantastic is that story? Aren't my parents the best? And you know who else is the best? You are, you magnificent bastard/bitch/Pisces, you! Did you do it in one 17-minute go? Did you stop and begin again so many times that you've grown a full chest-length beard since you started it? Did you have to FaceTime your own parents and read sections aloud to them while they continued to aim the phone camera either at the very top of their heads or right at their chins? Whatever it took to get you through, remember it! (By which I mean write it down in multiple places, because we don't remember shit. Goodbye, object permanence!)

And not to get all Obi-Wan Kedoobie on you, but this doesn't just go for reading. Living with ADHD is about finding what works for you and your loved ones and working it. You might have more pills in you than a pharmaceutical salesman's briefcase, or maybe you're rawdoggin' it with some mindfulness meditation and 6,000 weekly Google calendar notifications; that's between you and your wellness professional. (I personally draw the line at the guy who approaches you to do past-life regression at the clothing-optional beach, but you do you, sugar cookie. Just be safe and look for credentials.) The point of this little half-chapter here—of the story it told and of getting you to read it—was to remind both of us that our situations are never quite as helpless as they feel.

There's another reason I wanted to share this story with you, and, surprise, surprise, it has to do with ADHD.

One of the most common responses to an ADHD diagnosis—particularly an adult diagnosis, like mine—is a mourning period for the life that it now feels like you might have missed. It must be one of the most understandable and also least helpful feelings in the world. People become so frozen in their grief over hypothetical yesterdays that they lose out on real-life todays and tomorrows.

But a diagnosis doesn't change who you are; it brings new light and opens new horizons. In that sense, it's like my coming out to my parents. My mom and dad didn't start loving me, or knowing me, on the night I came out to them. But they knew me better now. Part of me that might have been a source of confusion or incomprehension to them before was now made accessible, and so by definition, they could show their love in even bigger ways. But that love was already there.

In the same way, the "you" that has masked and coped and scraped to get by until a diagnosis isn't some counterfeit version of you. All the strategies, the ingenious ways you've jerry-rigged for working around the fact that you live in a whole society designed for people whose brains work differently from yours ... they may not be helping you anymore, in the long run, but they started because of your smarts, and your self-care, and your instinct to survive. Because you are fucking tough. And you are worthy of love. And as you learn more about who you are and how your mind works, the ways to show that love will keep getting bigger.

WHAT DOES THIS MEAN FOR YOU?

- Having a neurodivergent brain doesn't mean you're lazy or "slow" or "too much." It means you process the world in a way that is unique to you. Our world is set up to cater to neurotypical brains, so it's no wonder that our processing time takes a bit longer. And we have a series of complex, sometimes beautiful workarounds to prove it.

- Reflecting on what your life was like, or what it could have been like, before your diagnosis, might be really painful. THIS IS NORMAL. You're here now, and we're in this together.

- Reading with ADHD can be an incredibly challenging skill. Do what works for you! Reading in small chunks; using a highlighter or taking notes in the margins to reflect and process as you need; or reading aloud to yourself, could potentially open things up for you. Just do you, queen!

CHOOSE YOUR OWN DISTRACTION

→ If you want to read about SWAT Team Tom's further adventures in allyship, this time in a secret mission to save a gay wedding, turn to page 97.

→ If you want to know how to play it cool during romantic courtship when hyperfixation has you zeroed in on dopamine but all you're really looking for is dope and a man, turn to page 90.

→ If you want to read about trying to start your own adult life on the other side of the country, without a diagnosis or much of a plan, keep reading …

Darcy Michael's Rejected ADHD Gay Bar Names

The Restless Leg

Impulse Control

Forgotten Glasses

The Assberg

EuroDivergence

Hard to Remember

Club Medz

Hyperfixationz

The Mood Swing

Object Spermanence

ADH+D

2.
ADHD & ADDICTION
DRUGS, DEBT, AND DANCING (EXCEPT NO DANCING)

I had made it through my school years—the time when a blossoming young male ADHDer is most likely to be spotted and pelted with handfuls of Ritalin or Adderall by a caring doctor and pharmacist—without being diagnosed. I was now entering young adulthood, a time in life that's tough for everybody—statistically even more fraught for queers—and extra dangerous for good measure if you have ADHD. What's the big danger, you ask? I'll give you a hint: if nobody in a white coat gives you any drugs, believe me—you will find some guy in white pants who will.

The science is pretty clear that gay teens and gay men are more likely to use "recreational" drugs (that is such a weird way to spell "self-medicate") or experience addiction than their straight peers.[1] My theory is that because our childhoods are so easy and full of social encouragement, we do this in order to level the playing field, but hey, I'm no scienteer.

But people with ADHD are even more unambiguously vulnerable to drug abuse (though arguably responsible for way fewer epic

---

1   https://www.theguardian.com/society/2003/nov/09/drugsandalcohol.drugs

club anthems?). Edward Hallowell, M.D., is a doctor with ADHD who also specializes in treating it, and while he has published with the same publisher as I have with this book, I'm about to quote from one of his books published with somebody else so there's no conflict of interest.[2] Hallowell says that "addictions of all kinds are five to ten times more common in people who have ADHD than in the general population."[3]

In my case, that meant that when an eighteen-year-old Darcy made the reverse journey eastward back to the province of his birth (I left the Volvo at home; I don't mean returning to the site of my birth quite that literally), he was statistically about as likely to remain drug-free as a one-hundred dollar bill in 1987 Miami.

Why was I in Toronto? I was half-heartedly pursuing my dream of being the next John Candy by taking classes at the legendary Second City. When I say half-hearted, what I mean is that I took exactly two classes at Second City and then quit. I told myself that this was because I was a lot funnier than everybody else there, and let's be frank: it's not impossible that this was a big part of the reason. It's taken many years for me to realize that traditional learning—even on the less-than-academic subject of sketch comedy—just doesn't fit my mold as a learner. Sure, I wasn't sitting in a classroom doing long division or ... I don't know, some other thing we learned to do in school. But a class is a class. It still required being told what to do, and when, and how, and that's not how I work. So, when somebody at Second City said, *"For this next scene, we need a location!"* I shouted, *"Somewhere else!"* and left.

---

2   My publishers would like to point out that Dr. Hallowell's non-DK books have been shown to cause wrist spasms, temporary finger paralysis, and acute reader's eye.

3   Hallowell & Ratey, *ADHD 2.0*, page 27. Sorry, these footnotes can't all be hilarious.

Instead of training me in the way of sketch comedy, Toronto became my initiation to grown-up gay culture (like sketch comedy, mainstream society only really became aware of gay culture in the sixties and seventies). Still, even here I was a slow learner. For instance, my nineteenth birthday was spent sitting on the stoop outside the famous Second Cup on Church Street because I had heard that its nickname was Second Cup Pick Me Up—but alas, I sat alone out front all night long ... it took me longer than it should have to figure out that people were fucking in the bathrooms of that coffee shop.

For my non-Canadian readers, nineteen is the legal drinking age in most of Canada so that means, yes, as of this particular birthday, I could have gone across the street to the bars to celebrate, but I was afraid—afraid I'd be TOO HOT FOR THEM TO HANDLE. And of course, by that I mean I get sweaty when I'm nervous, which makes me slippery and therefore one can't handle me. Comedy's best when I spell the jokes out, right? Maybe I should have stuck around for that third class at Second City.

Otherwise, Toronto was ecstasy. (Kids, that's what we used to call MDMA in the 1990s—true story.) I spent six months there flailing around the city trying enough drugs to keep me in statistical good standing with all of my demographic subgroups, while working at Sam the Record Man on Yonge Street just so I could buy discounted gay movies to watch in peace in my little studio apartment whose interior was hellishly lit from the outside by a giant neon sign that read—all too poignantly—The Heartbreak Hotel.

A short aside about Yonge Street—it's not short. Did you know it's the longest road in the world?[4] It spans a full 86 kilometers.

---

[4] Apparently Guinness World Records stopped listing it as the longest street in the world in 1999 after discovering it has been tacked onto the length of a provincial highway, thus proving once again everything in the nineties was just a little fucked up and weird.

(Again, for my American readers, that is approximately 1,000 miles.[5]) Or at least it felt like that when I finally landed my first audition and decided to walk from my apartment to the tryout to save on transit money. Now, to my young ADHD-riddled readers, this was before the internet was useful for anything beyond downloading low-res jpeg porn images in the blink of a half hour, so I could not Google Maps the location. Instead, I was stuck reading addresses on every block of the world's longest street and wondering why this was taking hours. Eventually, I arrived at this audition as I imagined I would have looked at the gay bar: fat, sweaty, and unprepared for what fate awaited me. The fate? I was a day late for the audition. Looking back on it now, I think a little undiagnosed neurodevelopmental issue might have come into play.

It's not the length of the walk that matters, but the girth. And this one was girth-shattering, because it was on this sweat-soaked trudge through the concrete jungle of Toronto that I made a deep realization. As I passed by a church that had a beautiful garden surrounded by long, lush grass, I found myself taking my shoes and socks off just to feel the earth under my feet and that's when I knew … I had stepped in dog shit.

I also knew it was time to move home to the West Coast. It was time to pack up and say, "Nice try, Toronto, but this little stoner hippy needs the cool breeze of the ocean, the soft touch of the grass and, well, to be honest the grass is better out West." Especially the smokable kind. I'm laughing in French right now. You know I'm talking about pot, right?

So I became what my dad termed "the Boomerang Child"—hey, can't spell B.C. without it!—and I moved back home with my parents. I was nineteen years old, with a slight aftertaste of independence, a raging case of horniness, a passion for the arts, and a

---

5   53.4 miles for those that don't understand comedy.

still-undiagnosed case of attention-deficit hyperactivity disorder. So I did exactly what you'd think I'd do: I got a job at a bank and bought a motorcycle.

Getting a job at a bank on the one hand and buying a motorcycle on the other is such a perfect combination of the safest possible thing to do and the most dangerous possible thing to do—so they basically cancel each other out. I should have been in a perfect equilibrium. Except that I made the "mistake" of not getting to the mail before my dad on the fateful day when he "accidentally" opened my credit card statement. Yes, that's right: mail tampering. My father, the retired cop, was now a criminal—oh, how the tides have changed! I'm deflecting here a bit because what he discovered, dear reader, was that I had racked up twenty-five thousand dollars in debt during my stay in Toronto. We'll talk about ADHD and money management in a later chapter, but part of it that many don't discuss publicly is that spending money is a dopamine fix that can't be beat.

But also, did you know that you have to pay back more than the minimum payment if you want your credit card debt to actually go down? Here I was thinking that the ten dollars a month I was sending to the Bank of Montreal was so easy and painless, the consumer society would never fail! And yes, in case you were wondering, this is the advice I was giving to clients at the bank I was employed at. So needless to say, I learned a few lessons that day—mainly, wow, can Dad's voice get loud! He's not angry, he's just "passionate."

It was also upon my return to Vancouver that I really found my love of weed. I remember being at my best friend Dustin's house smoking a bowl under a deck directly below his parents' bedroom window one night when I started to cough—and cough and cough and cough. These being the days before social distancing, through the hazy air Dustin whispered in a cottony voice, *"If you're going to puke, go over there."* And as I turned, and smiled, and just as the words, *"I'm not going to puke"* attempted to escape my throat, instead I proceeded to vomit all over both of us.

But that's what's great about weed—man, did we have a good laugh.

I started this chapter by telling you that those of us with ADHD are particularly vulnerable when it comes to drugs and addiction. Adults with ADHD have a higher prevalence of substance abuse disorder (15.2%) compared to those without ADHD (5.6%),[6] so vomit-soaked giggling aside, this all really is no laughing matter. People with ADHD turn to drugs and alcohol and other short-term addiction-fixes for the same reasons the general population does, only more so—plus throw in a few that are uniquely our own.

Sometimes it's a way of dealing with feeling like a "loser" because you can't seem to manage the things in life that are expected of you or that you expect of yourself. Sometimes it's a way of making the world feel more normal to a mind that's always jumping and racing—or if not normal, then at least bent and wacky on your own terms, for once. And sometimes it's as simple as chasing a dopamine hit that keeps getting more and more slippery.

If you find yourself struggling with addiction issues, be it with alcohol, marijuana, or other drugs or behaviors—be sure to reach out for some help. Even though my public persona comes across like I'm baked all the time, I'm proud to say I have a healthy relationship with drugs and alcohol. That's mainly because I don't drink anymore, and I started a rule in 2004 that I wasn't allowed to smoke weed until Oprah came on (which at the time was 4 p.m., and that really felt like a full business day to me, given that I'd already been up for four hours by then). All in all, it's been a good policy, but also I will admit that since Oprah went off the air, I'm

---

6   https://rehabsuk.com/blog/adhd-triples-risk-of-substance-abuse-but-it-doesn-t-have-to/

really fucking jonesin' for some smoke. I live for the Democratic National Convention every four years.

I had bad odds, statistically, but I was one of the lucky ones. By definition, not everybody is. I lost one of my best childhood friends to a cocaine addiction ... for a ten-year-old, he really did love his coke. (I do hate that I made that joke but if you haven't figured out by this point that comedy is how I cope, boy are you in for a fucking journey on this book.)

Jeff was a beautiful soul who was struck by an addiction that ultimately ended his life far, far too young at twenty-two years old. It breaks my heart to think about the life he could have had, the joy he should still be experiencing. So I think it's okay for us to take a break from the giggles to acknowledge that addiction is a fucking bitch and to remember that that bitch loves ADHDers ... so check in with yourself. I'm specifically talking to you—the person who's currently using this page to roll joints ...

WHAT DOES THIS MEAN FOR YOU?

- *"To thine own self be true."* I came up with that on my own! If you find yourself struggling in a particular learning environment or work style, don't be so quick to beat yourself up. The more you know about your own particular neuro-needs, the better you'll be able to adapt to life's challenges.

- Addiction is one of the hardest things that anyone can face, from the neurofabulous to the neuroadequate and everyone in between. Don't try to get through this alone. It's all love.

- Resist the urge to come up with your own pharmaceutical response to ADHD. I'm also not going to tell you what to take because guess what ... I'm a comedian from the internet. Trust your health care and mental health professionals. They don't make as much money as your drug dealers, but you have to admit that their waiting room art is more tasteful.

CHOOSE YOUR OWN DISTRACTION

→ If you want to hear about how dog ownership brought me closer to the internet, turn to page 192.

→ If you want to read about how I did not live any of this wisdom about substance use while I was filming a sitcom years later, back in Toronto, turn to page 131.

→ If you want to shake my family tree and see just how many apples fall out, keep reading ...

3.
ADHD & FAMILY
THE DAY THE APPLES TOOK FLIGHT

Listen, I'm probably not the first person to tell you that you shouldn't diagnose friends or family with ADHD or ASD (Autism Spectrum Disorders), but at the same time, secretly, between us friends ... it's kinda fun now and then to dip the sunglasses down the bridge of the nose, look at someone and go, "Oohhhhhh, hi friend—we have a lot in common."

Absolutely true story: I got some help with this book from my friend Charlie Demers, partly because we came up together on the Vancouver comedy scene and I know our values and senses of humor align, but also because he's written six and a half books (he co-wrote one, so he says that doesn't really count for full marks) and edited five others, all written by comedians. After I had sent him the first bunch of pages, he called me.

"Darcy, I've been going over everything you've sent me to read ..."

"Yeah?" I said with some trepidation.

"Dude ..." (I should probably note here that Charlie is straight.) *"Darcy, I think I might have ADHD."*

This genuinely caught me by surprise.

"Oh," I said. *"Charlie, I thought you knew you had it!"*

(Full disclosure: Some of the stuff in this book might be massaged a little to make it a little funnier or a little snappier. This is an almost verbatim transcription of a real conversation. Within a few months, Charlie had been diagnosed. Which was really great because then, any time he was late, he knew just what to say—suddenly I felt like Jer, and I did not like it!) I also want to note, this was included with his permission. I'm not outing anyone about their diagnosis ... or on that note, their sexuality ... *cough*, Dave, *cough*.

Is ADHD learned or genetic? Again, I'm not a doctor but I would say ... yes. Both. So sometimes, when I look back on my childhood with my parents, I can't help but think—hmmmm, so THAT'S where I get it from.

My parents worked hard, so very hard, to give us a great life. And I think they accomplished it. They were determined that we would have summers full of attention-grabbing events, like the time my dad and his buddies from the bomb squad decided that the hornet's nest in our backyard didn't need "an expert" because they were their own experts in their field. So ... they could just blow it up!

Which they did! Very successfully! And then, they called in other experts—known colloquially as "firemen"—to help put out the hedges that were quickly set ablaze and burnt away the entire privacy of our backyard. I'd like to file this piece of evidence under "impulse control issues." When your search for dopamine requires a call to emergency services, it may be time to take stock.

Then there was the time my mom decided, on a whim, that her precious Sesame Street–loving angels should have the opportunity to see the real Sesame Street in person. So with the station wagon packed to the tits with all the things we wouldn't actually need (*cough* ADHD-packing techniques *cough*—we'll get to those later), off on a road trip to Sesame Street we went. "C" is for kooky.

At some point during the drive from Toronto to New York—which I want to point out here is not short by any means—Mom saw an apple stand that was apparently just too good of a deal to pass up, and so she convinced my begrudging father to pull over the station wagon and proceeded to fill it even more with two full, giant bushels of apples. I was only four at the time and even to me, lacking any knowledge of cross-border fruit-transportation regulations, this did not seem in any way practical.

As we continued along on our own little PBS version of *National Lampoon's Vacation,* we finally made it to New York City. Now for you youngsters, it's important to know that New York in the eighties was way different! There was public urination, and the cocaine didn't have any fentanyl in it! WHAT A TIME TO BE ALIVE! Start spreading the news!

The other thing that was different about the eighties was that we didn't have Google Maps and, knowing my dad, we probably didn't have any paper maps either, so we simply zig-zagged through the streets of New York—in our apple-stuffed wood-paneled station wagon with three farting kids and two seething adults trying to find this magical place and ... it was not going well.

You see, road trips are ... a ticking time bomb for disaster. And I say this as someone whose father blew up a hornet's nest.

Sure, you get to drive by cool sights at 80 miles an hour. But the urge to kill whoever is beside you comes even faster than that.

After four hours of searching—which now, in retrospect, seems like miraculously little time given that we were more or less randomly driving around one of the world's most teeming metropolises—we finally found Sesame Street. We had arrived all of one hour before closing time, which, I will point out, is an 8:1 ratio of "driving from Pickering Ontario to see Sesame Street" to "actually being at Sesame Street."

But you see, dear reader, at this point us kids were exhausted and famished, and we couldn't possibly be expected to walk the full length of Sesame Street, so Mom asked Dad to get our little wooden wagon out of the trunk, because yes, of course, the little wooden wagon was riding in the big wood-paneled wagon the whole time. It was like a Russian nesting doll of eighties kitsch. At this point, my dad had reached his limit on this road trip. He was as tired and hungry as any of us were, but he also knew the terror he was absolutely unwilling to face—that of my mother not getting her way. So off he trekked to the back of the wagon to get the other wagon, and as he opened the trunk, as though he was in some golden-era silent-film comedy, both enormous bushels of totally unnecessary apples fell over onto him and started rolling everywhere in the parking lot.

He'd had it.

The apples had shaken him—yes—to his core.

And so, dad proceeded to surrender to what we like to call a "passionate moment" and just started chucking apples everywhere. I mean, picking up fallen apples and throwing them. Outside of Sesame Street. They were going into the car, he was whipping them at parking signs; if the Count had been anywhere in the vicinity, I have no doubt he would have taken 1-2-3 square in the temple.

While Dad continued single-mindedly with his fruity pitching practice, my mom calmly gathered her three cherubs into the all-important wooden wagon and simply proceeded to walk us toward the entrance, saying, *"Come, children, your father's crazy. Let's go find Big Bird."*

Now some might read this story and say, "But what does this have to do with ADHD?" And I would say, "Hmmm, I'm not entirely sure, but it is a nice way to find out if my parents read this book."

But it's also about the fact that things happen to us, repeatedly, but we forget. Then, we continue to repeat the pattern without even realizing it's a pattern, until it's too late. Until one day, when you're in your forties and you're writing a book and it's a week before you're about to head off on a road trip across the country with your husband and you think, *"Oh, shit ... maybe we should fly?"*

The road trips in our house continued for my entire childhood. No matter what we all thought about them, we were going on road trips.

And no matter what, they were ending with some sort of blow-up between all of us.

Like the time we were driving back from Palm Springs to Vancouver. To appreciate this story, you need to know that because my parents were on limited vacation time, when we went to Palm Springs, we would do the entire drive without stopping. It was twenty-two hours door to door. Dad would drive for eleven hours; then Mom would take over for a while; he got a few hours of sleep, and then he would get back to it. My brother and sister and I would just sit. And stare. There were no iPads, no TVs in the back of the front seats or swinging down from the ceiling. There was just John Denver on repeat for twenty-two hours. And farting.

One year, we were driving back through the Oregon mountain pass, and my dad was trying to get some sleep while Mom drove. Dad had to be at work three hours after we were scheduled to be at home and things were TENSE.

As my mom drove through the mountains, she had a habit of gunning it down the straightaways and then braking hard on the turns, so we were driving along in this herky-jerky motion for about twenty-five minutes before Dad finally lost it and screamed for her to pull over and switch with him. But this wasn't enough. He got into the driver's seat and proceeded to slam on the gas and then brake, slam and brake, mimicking her style as he screamed the ultimate insult: *"You drive like I fuck!"*

Or maybe the penultimate insult. The three preteens cowering in the back seat shoved our faces into pillows trying not to laugh at this vulgar outburst, as my mom puffed her own pillow and leaned it up against her window.

"That's funny," she said. *"I don't remember running out of gas."*

And then we rode in absolute silence the remaining eleven hours home. Not even John Denver was going to cap Mom's ruthless takedown of my father.

Bless. Did we remember this moment the next year, when we were packing the car up to return to Palm Springs? Yes. But did it stop us? No. Because undiagnosed ADHD knows no bounds.

So, what's the point of all this? When I introduced you to my parents in some of the first pages of this book, you caught a glimpse of how much they loved their kids. (Well, me; we're inferring love of my siblings.[1]) What these stories show is that, if we don't know what is going on with ourselves or with our loved ones—with their mental health, their neurodiversity, the parts of them that aren't as easy to spot as the noses on their faces or the apples in their hands—then even that love will struggle to make itself felt sometimes. And that goes just as much for our self-love (I'm being spiritual here; I don't mean the stuff you go blind from) as our love for each other.

These days, when Jer and I travel, we build in the room we know that each of us is going to need. ADHD packing is a bitch—so I start earlier than Jer, and I get to bring more luggage than him.

---

1   This inference is correct.

(Hey, I'm the one who pushes it through the airport, so don't look at me like that.) We factor in down time, and we don't schedule ourselves too close to the bone so we have a buffer when things go south.

I guess what I'm trying to say is ... I'm better than my parents.

Okay, well fuck, now for sure we'll know if they read it.

Love you Mom and Dad, but for the love of mother nature, learn to take a plane every now and then.

WHAT DOES THIS MEAN FOR YOU?

- Two things I never pack without: a checklist and a strict limit on the number of bags I'm allowed to bring. Okay, three things I never pack without if you count a mellow edible glow.

- Your family's shit is your shit, obviously, because they're your family. But it's also not your shit, because you're you. Try to remember that just because your family has been struggling with something for more than a generation doesn't mean you're doomed—it means you have context.

CHOOSE YOUR OWN DISTRACTION

→ If you want to hear about how I failed to book a sitcom role playing a gay character written for me, turn to page 118.

→ If you want to learn how I got past all my family's travel hangups, conquered my fear of credit card debt, and went to Europe without technically having the money to do it, turn to page 175.

→ If you want to know how I found true love, keep reading ...

(See, that got even YOUR attention!)

NEUROFABULOUSNESS THROUGH THE GENERATIONS

As both someone with ADHD and a practicing homosexual (you know I say practicing, but honestly, I nailed it years ago), I happen to belong to the two groups that people are most likely to wonder aloud about how it happened while pretending not to be disappointed about it. The very phrase "nature versus nurture" was pretty much invented so your uncle could share his meditations on Ritalin and butt sex out loud at social gatherings. ADHD has been blamed on everything from food dye to video games, while for many years my mom was convinced that I was gay because she let me serve fruit punch instead of root beer at my seventh birthday party. But as with human sexuality, growing bodies of research are increasingly pointing toward the fact that when it comes to neuro-wiring, nature just makes a bunch of different kinds of people, and that there is an important genetic dimension to ADHD. Let's see if this trip up the branches of the Michael family tree bears any of that out!

Darsy the Bestoned (1131-1187)

A jester in the court of King Henry II, Darsy's tales of ribaldry and forgetfulness were said to bring great pleasure to the royals and their coterie. In one of his most popular routines, Darsy would inhale vast quantities of smoke that was said to be incense taken from the royal chapel, although none was ever reported missing. The jester's inability to remember the names of local aristocrats and visiting dignitaries was said to please King Henry greatly. Sadly, Darsy was put to death in 1187 for trying to fuck the future King Richard the Lionheart.

Darkley "Bear Beard" Myckal (1552-1589)

One of Queen Elizabeth I's anti-Spanish privateers, Bear Beard's career as a pirate was cut short when, according to the ship's log, he was supposed to be scanning the horizon for hours in the crow's nest but was instead caught "polishing his peg." There is no indication whether this was a euphemism. Bear Beard's defiant last words as he walked the plank still haunt us down through the centuries: "You bitches have scurvy, but I'm just scurvaceous!"

"Lost Guns" Darson Mickael (1820-1890)

Broadly considered the least efficient cowboy on the mesa, Lost Guns Darson had a reputation for hyperfixating while branding a cow, obsessing so much on placement and symmetry that he could hold up an entire cattle drive for hours. Struggles with object permanence also left Lost Guns easy prey for rustlers. He was, however, admired for his generosity, famously willing to "share his saddle with any lonesome cowpoke under the stars."

Lieutenant D. M. Michael (1880-1916)

Beloved of the soldiers who served under him in the trenches, who cited his great bravery and deep, warm affection, Lieutenant Michael succumbed to an extreme case of Rejection Sensitive Dysphoria when he became utterly convinced that the Germans didn't like him.

Darlene Michael (1919-1961)

Bored to stupefaction by her upbringing in a Southern Ontario farming town, Darlene thrilled to the call during WWII for young women to enter the industrial workforce supplying armaments, vehicles, and materiel. Said to finally be able to pay attention for the first time in her life, she was riveted by riveting. Darlene was also a fixture at auxiliary dances for soldiers on leave and is reported to have accomplished what the Axis powers couldn't and put the entire Canadian army on its back.

Well, I hope you enjoyed that journey through the branches of my family tree as much as I enjoyed producing DNA to send to Ancestry.com. (Oh grow up, I wiped it off a bong, I'm not an animal!) We didn't even get to talk about some of my favorite relatives, like the late-eighteenth century aristocrat Lord Darcy Michaelbottom (who is not to be confused with the author of this book, Lord Darcy Michael Domtop).

4.
ADHD & LOVE
HOW TO TAKE IT SLOW WHEN YOUR MIND MOVES FAST, FAST, FAST

Okay, at this point you're a foreword, an introduction, and three full chapters into a book about ADHD—I mean, if you're reading it in order. It could be that this is the first sentence of the book that you're reading. Or this one. Probably less likely to be this one, given its placement in the paragraph. But you get what I mean. If you're just joining our program, *Welcome.* My name is Darcy and I'm gay/stoned/distracted. You're all caught up—which in hindsight doesn't speak well for those previous chapters.

So, how have I done it? How did I write all the pages you've now got in your left hand despite my tendency to follow whatever comes into my line of vision with the loyalty of a baby duck following its mama?

Taking a step back, how have I been more-or-less successfully navigating life for the past several years, celebrating important milestones in parenting, business, creativity, romance, and Golden Retriever beach rock procurement? (I know my online persona is "flaky pothead with a tendency toward zoning out," but if we could just get real for a second here—if people saw how hard I actually work on any given day, our brand would dissolve as quickly as a sugar cube in the pocket of DJ Khaled's sauna suit.)

So, how did I do it? The answer, like all good things, is very gay: I found my ADHD Wrangler, and I never let him go.

I think it's time we all meet Jer.

(By the way, he's going to be so pissed that he doesn't show up until Chapter 4. So, if anybody asks, this is the preface.)

Given that millions of people now watch the intimacies of our life together every day on the internet, you may be surprised to learn that we met twenty-two years ago ...

... on the internet.

That's right, I guess we're finally getting into the horny stuff: MSN Messenger. Now for you kids too young to know this beautiful reference, I want you to imagine yourself back in the George W. Bush era, and you just got home from watching *My Big Fat Greek Wedding*. Let's say you wanted to text your friend to speculate on what a possible sequel might entail—would the wedding be fatter? Greeker? Might the wedding be, illegally, to another woman? To send that text, you would fire up your computer like a lawnmower and wait for it to connect to the internet. (Hopefully no one at your house was on the phone, because if so, you'd have to wait.) Then you'd just have to hope that friend was online at the exact same moment you were, and then BOOM, you'd send them a message. The era of "instant to five or fifteen minutes later" connection had arrived!

Now that you have a sense of the technology involved, let me set the scene in terms of personnel. I was twenty-one years old; I was still chubby, I was starting to go bald, and to compensate, my body was producing chest hair at a rate that my internal twink was absolutely disgusted by. (Now there's a memoir—*I Swallowed My*

Own Twinkie: The Darcy Michael Story.) Being, as previously mentioned, both horny and easily distracted, I had also sort of fucked my way around my circle of friends, and so there I was, just sort of weary and worn out and looking for my next dopamine hit.

At the time, I was working at a call center for a company called RezRez—which, despite our society's tendency to take stupidly named companies and inflate their value to billions and billions of dollars, no longer seems to be going strong from what I can tell. But at the time, we helped people book overpriced vacations to British Columbia's ski paradise peaks at Whistler/Blackcomb. My job at the time was as a customer care manager. Yes, that's right. If you were an affluent hill bunny and something went horribly wrong with your fancy ski vacation and you called in to speak to a manager, my sultry voice would come onto the line to let you know that everything was going to be okay. And by everything being okay, I mean I would usually just put you on hold while I investigated your situation by going outside to smoke a joint with my friends before eventually remembering that someone was on hold and just gently hanging up on you. ADHD Ski Trip Assistance: It's All Downhill from Here!™

"Darcy, why does this matter in a book about ADHD?!" the reader may be asking themself. Full disclosure, the publisher asked the same question when they read this! And sure, I guess from some angles it's a fair question. But really, at this point you could ask yourself why any new book about ADHD in an already-oversaturated content landscape full of hucksters and overnight experts matters? And while we're at it, in a social framework without a clear set of guiding metaphysical values, why does life matter? (For the record the publisher hated the second-to-last question, and that last question just made them quiet and sad.)

Well, I can't answer any of those things, but what I can say is that knowing I worked at RezRez is an important flex for me because 1) this was my last real job, and 2) it was at this job that one of my coworkers told me about a new website for connecting with people online. Part of a crop of popular new sites that would transform the attention economy of both neurodivergents and neurotypicals alike, you will no doubt nod along in recognition as I tell you that the social networking site my coworker told me about was called Face …

… -Pic.com. Good ol' Face-Pic.com, obviously. Why, what did you think I was going to say?

Now, Face-Pic.com was essentially—GASP IN 2002 HORROR—an online dating site. I have to pause here and explain to anyone who doesn't leave silver curlies on the soap that at the beginning of this century (a century that will almost certainly end with a Canadian prime minister whose parents met online and saw each other's privates on their phones before seeing them in person), online dating was looked at askance and with suspicion by most people. A website. To meet HUMANS. What is this chaos you speak of?!

But as with fashion, music, and Subaru maintenance (thanks, lesbians!), gay people were pioneers in online hooking up. Maybe it was the centuries of taking our life in our hands every time we wanted to start flirting in person, maybe it was 'cuz we're tech savvy. Really it's anybody's guess.

But you know me—I was always looking for a hit of my two favorite D's (one of them is dopamine). So sure enough, I signed up for Face-Pic.com. It was a simple site; you just entered your picture, name, location, and birth sign because it was clearly created by a witch trying to do identity theft. I spent six and a half hours uploading my heavily pixelated 2-inch by 2-inch picture, slapped on my name and my Aries birth sign, and added that I lived in Whistler. *"But Darcy,"* I can already hear you saying, *"Did you really live in Whistler? You're not even Australian!"* I did not. I just thought it was cool and figured that this way none of the weird internet murderers could find me in my hometown of Lynn Valley. (Man, it's quaint to remember a time when "internet murderer" was its own separate subset of murderers. Like "internet famous"—as opposed to where, may I ask? In books? Well, good news, guess what you're holding, creep!)

The real magic of Face-Pic.com was that it connected to your MSN Messenger account. (And yes, you smug young assholes, I realize that this sentence reads something like, "The real magic of the horse and buggy was that it facilitated the delivery of scarlet fever poultices." We get it, you're immortal!) And lo and behold, I started chatting with this guy named Jeremy.

Luckily for Jer and me, I sat at a computer not helping people for eight hours a day, so I would just be around the chat while he was at home from college doing homework. We talked for hours a day online, just chatting about life. He had a baby, and this was so weird to me. I really couldn't comprehend a gay man having a child at our age. (Or any age, thanks to my limited sex education class with our gym teacher Mr. Wilson ... I'll never forget him just eating the banana and saying, "you'll figure it out boys"—though I appreciate his commitment to serotonin intake.) So one time, during these endless conversations with Jer, I asked him flat out why he had a baby.

Why hadn't they, y'know ... I dunno, maybe, just ... why didn't they ... well ... you know? And he said it was God's way of giving him a baby before he realized who he was. *WHAT?!* And *SWOON!*

As a punk antiestablishment know-it-all queer call center manager (it's a cliché for a reason), I was immediately thrown by a gay man referencing God. What is this? Is this confusion on my part? Can someone have a baby, believe in God, AND be gay? He's practically straight! Can you see my boner through the page? And thus, Jer's nickname around my cubicle quickly became "Jesus Lovin' Baby Maker." Why? Because I was (and still am) a fucking moron with no depth. And hey, you bought a book by me, so what's that say about you?!

Regardless, I was intrigued and at this point I just needed to see this guy face to face, with no pic or .com. I was about to suggest we *meet in person*. Now, while you're reading this book and potentially scrolling Grindr or Tinder or Christian Mingle without a care in the world about meeting a stranger for some back-alley fuckery, I have to remind you that in 2002's big, fat, Greek world, this was *unheard* of.

But he agreed.

When I told my friends that I had set up a date with the Jesus Lovin' Baby Maker, the gay gasps could be heard around the world ... or at least around my cubicle.

My friends Maureen and Zach were absolutely terrified that I was going to get gay bashed, or worse—fall in love. They insisted on being at the restaurant for my first date, just sitting like little spies at a table nearby so that they could keep a queer eye on this potentially murderous religious zealot.

(Now, if Jer were here, he'd do an audible eye roll—not ideal for this setting, but it'll be great for the audiobook—and say something like, *"I have never been religious. I made one comment on a chat board twenty-two years ago about how things in life happen for a reason, but my little hyperfixater found something to cling to—and if Darcy loves anything, it's a stupid nickname. Not that you can't be religious and queer and a dad."* To which I would reply, *"Well, if you're not religious, then why was our first date at the Jupiter Café, clearly a tribute to the Roman gods? Or did you just want to worship a gas giant?"* and he would say *"Darcy!"* and then we'd be done filming for the whole day.)

The fact is, I was terrified to meet him. There I was, an hour early sitting at Jupiter Café in the Davie Village, a cute little martini bar with a big patio, allowing me to plot multiple escape routes. And then right on time, off of Face-Pic.com and into real life walks my little raver boy ... with bright red hair spiked with what I can only assume was about seventeen pounds of Dippity Do and a—wait for it—*CHIN STRAP BEARD?!!*

Now, wait just a goddamn minute ...

Where was the twink I'd been talking to online for months and months? Well, he was hidden beneath the fine dark black line of hair grasping along his chiseled jawline. I can still remember the giant pants and tiny gray coat that he was wearing. We hugged, sat down, and ordered espresso martinis. Hours went by, but this wasn't ADHD time blindness. (We'll get to that.) There was something here; there was something happening to me that would take me years to understand, but now, looking back at it, I can see that it happened from the get-go.

My leg stopped bouncing.

My heart was steady.

My brain was focused.

My breathing deepened and slowed.

What devilish sorcery was this Jesus Lovin' Baby Maker working on me?

What was this?

WHAT DOES THIS MEAN FOR YOU?

- In the initial stages of a new relationship or courtship, stay aware of the way your tendency to hyperfixate (and/or to drop it just as quickly) might play out with your new crush, and how it will affect them.

- SET YOUR FUCKING ALARM! Don't miss the date that might land you your Jer.

CHOOSE YOUR OWN DISTRACTION

→ If you want to know what was happening with my body, keep reading ...

→ If you want to know what was happening with my mind, keep reading ...

→ If you want to know how I found true love, just keep fucking reading ...

SPEND YOUR INTERCHAPTER CLIFFHANGER TIME PRODUCTIVELY!

Avoid the dreaded Sit Pit with this complimentary word jumble![1]

As many ADHDers know, if the day is cut up into the wrong sizes or shapes, it is—to use the medical term—fucked. Let's say I have a morning Zoom meeting that ends at 11:30 a.m., followed by a doctor's appointment at 2:45 p.m. Well, the intervening three hours and fifteen minutes will be a dead-air blank space in which nothing is accomplished aside from me sitting and staring off into the middle distance (the "Sit Pit"), unless I remember to set myself small, clearly defined, easy-to-accomplish tasks and goals for the interstitial time. Maybe I could make sixty-five 3-minute eggs? Or watch *The Godfather III* and then one episode of *The King of Queens*, if for some reason I was angry at myself. The point is, the time has to be filled deliberately or else it will be lost to sands of ... well, fuck ... time.

So if for some reason you're not able to read both chapters of our ADHD love story in one go, please engage yourself with this complimentary Darcy & Jer Jumble![2]

---

1   Included in price of book.

2   Again, you have technically paid for it already.

```
M X Z Q V I S D C M
E P P U C F L O B P
D L E V H B G N U E
S A A D H D B K S X
R N N B U D T E Y T
D T Q X I M Q Y A M
D S N V T S J G O G
T B X P O P Q U I Z
F Y V U I L E T P M
U K H T H C L R Y Y
```

Answers: busy, donkey, thc, pop quiz, meds, adhd, plants, lgbtq. (It's not really fair to put so many sets of initials in a jumble, sorry.) Wow, look at you learning to turn a book upside down! I had to watch seven YouTube tutorials on how to flip this word box. And one video on how to change a boxcutter blade because it came up as a suggested video, and honestly, it's a good thing to know!

5.
ADHD & COURTSHIP
THE COURTSHIP OF GRACE'S FATHER(S)

It was *calm*. That's what I was feeling. I didn't know it then, but I know it now. When Jer came into my life and sat across from me, I had found the calm eye to my storm. I had found someone who made me feel ... at ease.

Now, is this the heart-racing excitement that infatuation, sexual attraction, and even love is supposed to be? Maybe not for some, but for me it was—the peace was thrilling.

Dr. Sheva Rajaee, a specialist who treats anxiety and OCD, particularly in relation to romantic attachments, talks about the physical language we often use to describe what's supposed to be "true love," like butterflies in the stomach.[1] Like a pounding heart or weak knees, they're also the symptoms of an anxiety attack.

But those aren't the feelings you have when you feel safe and at home.

Those weren't the feelings I was having then.

This was even better than that.

---

1   https://www.youtube.com/watch?v=y8Wh5ezL4c0

It was different, so I wanted to treat it differently.

After our drinks, I bid Jer adieu with a simple, chaste kiss on the cheek. (And his face cheek, to boot! I know, how very hetero of us.)

All of this was strange. I didn't know how to process the idea that I liked this weird-bearded, Jesus-lovin', baby-making raver twink so much that ... I didn't go home with him after. Because I wanted it to be special? Barf.

But special it was—we spent months just dating. The beard was gone by date 2, so I was locked in at that point.

SIDE BAER
I, on the other hand, did not love date 3, when he showed up all preppy dressed in a golf shirt and carrying a purse ...

IT WASN'T A PURSE! It was a Mountain Equipment Co-Op side-bag, and it was very au courant in 2002.

No, it wasn't.

It's a book, Jer—not a script for community theater. Less dialogue, more focus!

MOVING ON. Here's the thing: we both agreed we wanted to take things slow. And that's not always easy for people with ADHD. Everybody knows what it's like to get swept up in a crush. But with the ADHD brain's tendency to lock into hyperfixation, the early stages of love can sometimes be a little intense. Sometimes the actions of head-over-heels ADHDers have even been mistaken for "love bombing." Now, I thought "love bombing" was just a handy catch-all euphemism for American foreign policy, but it turns out it's a little more complicated than that. Love bombing is a subtle form of manipulation that comes from being not-so-subtle about declarations of love, fast and heavy off the top, in a way that's meant to be disorienting. But sometimes the hyperfixated ADHD lover can act in ways that mirror love bombing pretty closely. Somebody wrote an article about it for *Vice*;[2] I did my best to read almost all of it, but you know me—like the saddest little calf on the dairy farm, I was born to skim.

The fact is, like with pretty much everybody, romantic relationships where ADHD is present are a mixed bag. And don't just ask me, ask *Psychology Today*. (Today at the time I'm writing this; it'll be *Psychology a Little While Ago* by the time you read this.) We can pivot from hyperfixation to distracted, inattentive, and late all the time—then compensate with extraordinary sex drives and creative lovemaking.[3] Hey, don't shoot the messenger—I'm just telling you what today's psychologists are saying.

We didn't know any of this when we started dating. But by some lucky Aries fluke or by the guiding hand of the providence that made a baby through my Jesus-lovin' raver twink, we knew to take things slowly. For our sake, and for the sake of the fact that Jer was busy with school, working as a waiter, and raising his—soon to be our—daughter Grace.[4] That, plus I was sort of freaked out

---

2 https://www.vice.com/en/article/hyperfixation-love-bombing-adhd-relationships/

3 https://www.psychologytoday.com/ca/basics/adhd/adhd-and-relationships

4 Spoiler!

about meeting his kid, so we wanted to wait until it was something we knew was more than just dates ...

And then we fucked.

SIDE BAER

DARCY MICHAEL!

Yeah, baby—reader, we did it gooooooooood.

 This is not what the book is about! We're skipping ahead to when you met Grace. You smutty little monster.

Ugh, sex always leads to parenthood with you— you're such a breeder.

I met Grace one day at the restaurant Jer worked at ... ABC Country Restaurant in Ladner, BC. If you want to get a feel for the setting in which I, a very large, conspicuous, bearded man, was about to meet my boyfriend's kid, let me paint a picture. If a Republican presidential candidate scouting locations for a commercial shoot walked into the ABC Country Restaurant in Ladner, BC, in 2002 he would say, *"I'm sorry, this place is just a little too conservative for me—and hey, a little diversity wouldn't kill you guys."* Don't get me wrong, I would come to love Ladner. But at the time it felt like going back in time. It was ... quaint?

That day, I remember Grace being so shy and so confused—guess she gets that from her dad. I was just grateful she didn't have a fucking chinstrap beard.

She didn't really want to talk much—she was maybe three at this point? I don't remember exactly because, well ... drugs.

But I do remember thinking, "Man, I gotta get this kid to like me or I'm fucking toast." (At the time I didn't know I was celiac, therefore I didn't even realize what a perfect symbol of lethal danger toast was.)

I should note that my meeting with Grace was happening while Jer was working a shift. So she was there to hang out with me for a period of several hours, and what the fuck—err, what the heck—am I going to talk to a three-year-old about for several hours?!

So I swung big. I said to her, *"Tables are so boring. I love hats; let's sit underneath the table like it's our hat."* Truthfully, it was still so early on in our relationship I didn't want Jer to see me eating Grace's chicken fingers. It was better that he learn about that over time. So there's Jer floating around the restaurant serving tables as Grace and I ate chicken fingers and colored outside the lines on Jer's extra notepads under the table.

The burst of outside-the-box, childlike ADHD thinking had bought me some time and goodwill. She was opening up to me as a possibility, but we weren't there yet.

Until it happened: I said something funny, and she laughed. I smiled, because I had the little fucker in the palm of my hand ... but the smile dissolved when I realized that it was the other way around; she had me in hers. Her face lit up with the heartbreaker smile that was so very much hers and so very much her father's at the same time, and it hit me like a fist in the stomach. There were those butterflies. Fuck. Shit. Fuck. Fuck. This was the start.

I was about to fall in love with two of the kindest, gentlest souls I'd ever meet.

Then she dropped a chicken finger onto the carpet and started to cry the loudest cry I'd ever heard and then I thought: Fuck. Shit. Fuck. Fuck. Kids are such a buzzkill.

The rest is an absolute blur—we went in so fast even my lesbian friends thought we should slow down the U-Haul to avoid a speeding ticket. But I couldn't stop; the hyperfixation train was full speed ahead to family-building town. I moved from my only halfway quaint little boomerang life living with parents in Lynn Valley to the all-the-way quaint land that time forgot: Ladner, BC.

Now if you want to truly understand Ladner, watch every episode of *Gilmore Girls*, because I had moved to Stars Hollow. (Only instead of the cute guy who has a daughter from a previous relationship making good coffee for you in his diner, he fucks you in the apartment you share.) It felt like every weekend in this little fishing and farming village they had some sort of parade happening. I swear one parade was just called "parade" and the people just walked and waved—at themselves in the reflection of the windows of the four storefronts.

What was this place? I don't know, but I do know that being gay in a small town was—well, the closest thing we had to a pride parade was when Jer and I checked the mail at the same time.

After years of learning about various things to do with my neurodiversity, one of my favorites is a thing called *body doubling*. (Not as exciting as it sounds, but ultimately even more enriching than what you're picturing.) Body doubling literally just means having someone in the room with you. It can help someone like me when I'm finishing a task or to have someone to bounce ideas off of—it helps with productivity for people like me. But with Jer, the doubling isn't some productivity life hack or shortcut for getting through a to-do list. His presence makes me even more who I am.

> **SIDE BAER**
> You're very sweet. Okay, I won't grow the chin-strap back.

We were living in our idyllic little hamlet with Grace staying on the weekends and me commuting ninety minutes each way, five days a week to my call center job in North Vancouver and Jer going to school full time, working part time and raising a kid ... and as you can imagine, it was heaven. Oh my days, I had it all. I was so happy the dopamine machine was in overdrive.

And then, because standing still is not an option for ADHD man nor society itself, we had a date with gay marriage.

WHAT DOES THIS MEAN FOR YOU?

The ADHD brain has a tendency to work in overdrive. When it comes to love and dating, the ideal partner will be able to help you slow down and enjoy the scenery.

CHOOSE YOUR OWN DISTRACTION

→ If you want to read how we took body doubling to the next level, then around the world, first take your head out of the gutter, then turn to page 218.

→ If you want to learn about object permanence and how I almost blew it with Jer—and the email that saved us—turn to page 141.

6.
ADHD & MARRIAGE
WHEN I WAS YOUR AGE, WE HAD TO WALK UPHILL BOTH WAYS TO GET GAY-MARRIED

You know, time is a funny thing. In his famous autobiography *Confessions*, Saint Augustine said, *"What, then, is time? If no one asks me, I know what it is. If I wish to explain it to him who asks me, I do not know."* (I tried to use this quote to prove to my editor that the very first guy to write a book about himself couldn't deal with deadlines, but it went nowhere.) Let's talk for a minute about time and, specifically, how ADHD and time are not linear. For instance, I've barely started talking about this and I already feel like I've been droning on about this subject for far too long. That said, I could talk about plants for days and it'll feel like mere seconds have gone by. (The editor also made me cut the paragraphs I inserted about plants and I'm still having a tough time with it.)

That same elastic relationship with time goes for romance and ADHD—things either just work and go "U-Haul lesbian" or they don't, and the dopamine is drained like a hot tub after an orgy: with deep feelings of regret. Or with even deeper regret if you forget to drain the hot tub after an orgy.

But time can be funny in other ways, too. For instance, global civilization can go chugging along for several thousand years with a basic understanding that relationships between homosexuals should be either politely ignored and benignly tolerated or violently hunted down by the state and/or youth athletic coaches, and everything in between. And then all of a sudden—not even ten years after your principal told you that you had to take a throuple to the prom because a boyfriend wasn't an option—not long after you've met the love of your life, your province becomes one of the first jurisdictions in the world to legalize same-sex marriage.

In 2003, two years before it would become the law of the land across Canada, two men named Michael married each other in Toronto. Obviously, this set a huge precedent: because so many couples had the same first names, married gays would almost never take each other's last names.

I had never thought about getting married because getting married had never been an option. Marriage was something I had never wanted, and I think a lot of that was because I wasn't afforded the ability to dream about it. We just wanted to be able to exist without fear of being gay bashed. But in the summer of 2003, a mere six months after meeting each other, Jer and I got engaged. For you heterosexuals that might seem like ADHD impulsivity, but the homos reading know that in gay years we were practically at our silver jubilee.

But ADHD did shape almost every aspect of the proposal, the wedding, and the marriage. Me being the super romantic and carefree partner who completed Jer's button-down life, I had this incredible plan to propose to Jer on the beach at sunset.

First, I had to pick up his ring—a ring we couldn't afford to buy, incidentally, even though it was only two-hundred dollars. (Shockingly, it eventually turned his finger green. Thank you, Hudson's Bay! You had a flawless history until that ring.)

I thought all my plans were airtight. In order to pick up the ring, I needed an excuse to leave Jer at home that day so, brilliantly, I did what any normal, mentally sound person would do: I picked a fight about him being a slob and gaslit my way right out the door so he could sit and think about what he did wrong.

The entire time I was gone to pick up the ring, I felt terrible because it had been our first fight and I'd left poor little Jeremy to stew about it for hours while I drove into the big city of Vancouver to pick up his toxic engagement ring.

All my romantic, carefully laid plans fell by the wayside when I came home and saw my sweet Jeremy, still worried. (Although not worried enough to have cleaned up any of the shit I'd complained about five hours earlier; those video games ain't gonna play themselves.) My undiagnosed ADHD bullied its way to the front of my brain, shoving aside my thoughtful proposal idea, and instead, I followed the dopamine right then and there. I explained to my man—surrounded by his filth—that the idea of him and I *ever* being apart is something I couldn't have and didn't want. I got down on one knee, right onto a Styrofoam take-out container, and asked Jeremy to be my husband.

Until that moment he'd been convinced that I was breaking up with him, so Jer was downright shocked when he stammered and said, *"I'm a slob!"*

"I know you are, but you're my slob," I responded, and like that, we were two slobbery gay crying messes. We had found our family.

In 2004, our home province of British Columbia officially legalized gay marriage, joining the growing list of places where queers could now throw their future away TOGETHER. *Bless.*

But us ADHDers aren't the only people time plays tricks on. Time moves differently for everybody. Too slow for some. And then some people think it's moving too fast for them.

Jer's mom struggled with supporting same-sex marriage. It was all coming too fast and, in the days leading up to the wedding, we didn't know if she was going to be there with us. She didn't know if she was going to be there with us.

We actually didn't find out this next part until about ten years after the wedding, when my mother-in-law let it slip out. We were talking about our wedding week and she said something about how she needed to thank my dad for it all.

Jer and I both stopped dead in our tracks, confused. *I'm sorry what?* She tried to clam back up, but after some poking and prodding finally admitted that my dad—my big, tough, don't-talk-about-feelings retired-cop dad—had showed up the week of our wedding at Jer's mom's house. There, he had said to her, *"You don't have to like what they're doing, but you have two choices—one, you show up to that wedding with a smile on your face and be in their lives, or two, you don't go and that's it. You can't be one foot in and one foot out. These boys love each other and we're gonna be there to support them whether we get it or not."*

And she was there.

SIDE BAER

My mom called me the day after our wedding to say how much fun she had and how overwhelmed she was by the amount of love that was being shared. She's been our biggest champion ever since, and for that I guess we have Darcy's dad to thank.

Okay, well first of all, you've really gotta stop bursting into the main narrative of the book like that; this isn't a podcast, dude. Secondly, don't give my dad all the credit, Jer, or he's gonna expect royalties for this story. But yes, it was shocking for me to hear that story from your mom all those years later, and also, somehow, not surprising at all. My dad has always understood what his role as a dad should be, and that is to show up.

Whereas my role was to be not only one of the grooms but also ADHD party planner. Event planning is not the natural arena of excellence for the ADHDer—way too many concrete details to follow through on—although it does provide a lot of room to get cute and creative. We got married on a little island outside of Ladner called Deas Island. The island has a cute little schoolhouse that we used for the speeches and dinner, but our ceremony took place outside in the forest with tiki torches (before their fascist associations, I promise). Grace stood up with the two of us as we said our vows in front of all the casually dressed friends and family who had been instructed to bring their own chairs if they didn't want to sit on the dirt.

There was supposed to have been about 75 people at our wedding but, neurofabulous impulse control being what it is, in the weeks leading up to the day the guest list kept growing until we landed at around 140 people—easily 40 of whom neither Jer nor I can name when looking at photos now, but I felt it was fun to just invite anyone I met leading up to it. You wanna come to a gay wedding? Come! Plus, in those still-early days, I figured there was a chance of protestors showing up, and I wanted strength in numbers ... so yes, a large majority of the guests were lesbians.

After the reception, Jer and I went home to discover our wedding party had stacked up all our gifts like a pyramid in the center of our living room, and because I love to chase the dopamine, before Jer and I could even consummate our vows, we were ripping open gifts and laughing away.

The next morning when our families arrived for what they called "the gift opening," they were pretty pissed. They were even less impressed that we hadn't made any notes about who had given us what. That's when Jer and I learned that you're supposed to thank people for their specific gifts in a card. I had undiagnosed ADHD; I don't know what Jer's excuse was. So if you were at our wedding, you're welcome for the generic thank you card. We tolerate you.

Anyway, the biggest wedding present was something Jer got us. Well, me. And it wasn't until a few days after the wedding. But while I'd been standing at the front of the Deas Island schoolhouse, making a toast and getting pretty huge laughs, my new husband had seen something special. He'd been quietly thinking that it might be good for me to focus my funny on something other than just shocking my coworkers with sass. So Jeremy Baer, my lawfully wedded husband, signed me up for a stand-up comedy class. And thus began his obsession with wanting to make me work.

WHAT DOES THIS MEAN FOR YOU?

Planning large-scale events, like weddings, is not always easy for neurodiverse thinkers—we tend to get lost in the details. Rely on your go-to coping mechanisms and take things one step at a time. Record everything so you can refer back to it!

CHOOSE YOUR OWN DISTRACTION

- → If you want to read how I first met Jer, turn to page 79.
- → If you want the sordid highlights of my prediagnosis stand-up comedy career, turn to page 105.
- → If you want to learn how I fought the ADHD odds to become a career-focused dude (BEING A COMEDIAN IS A CAREER, MOM!), keep reading ...

Classes Jer Wishes He'd Bought Darcy Instead of the Comedy Class, in Retrospect

House Plant Management: How Not to Re-Wild Your Living Room

Baggage-Packing for the Intermediate Traveler

Post-Retriever Lawn Repair

Hockey Fundamentals for the Canadian House-Spouse

Taking It Down a Notch for Beginners

The Days of the Week: A User's Guide

Bong Hydrodynamics

Intermediate Taking It Down a Notch

Playsuit Laundering

Where's My Car?: How to Find Where You Left Your Car for Beginners

Industrial Manscaping

7.
ADHD, CREATIVITY & REJECTION
UNTITLED OPRAH PROJECT

I think it's pretty fair to say that everybody wants to express themselves, and nobody particularly enjoys taking criticism. Today's comedians can often be heard complaining about how modern audiences are way too sensitive and reactive, and I can totally relate! I once had a crowd that wanted to beat the shit out of me just because they found out I liked cock! Ah, gay bashing: when "cancel culture" means a trip to the emergency room.

I was on tour in a small town that shall remain nameless, though I will say it rhymes with "Medicine Hat, Alberta." Things were going pretty smoothly as I was performing my usual opening ten minutes' worth of jokes about weed before I would out myself to the audience in a bit I liked to call Undercover Fag: "Surprise! We're everywhere!" And yes, in some small towns it caught some of the audience off guard, as it did on this particular night; but for the first time in my illustrious five-year comedy career, I wasn't just being heckled about the jokes. A posse of skinhead-looking fellas—maybe from the local Rotary Club or Lions, I really can't say—were pretty fucking mad that I had duped them into liking my weed jokes under false pretenses, only to discover that they'd been giggling with a gay man in front of all their friends. Thankfully, management kicked the hooligan yokels out of the venue for disrupting the show, which doesn't always happen on the road. So, all good, right? No. All is really not good.

They waited for me in the parking lot. Now listen, I'm great in a lot of situations: baby shower, coastal big city dispensary, Pride parade buffet afterparty. Dark backwoods parking lots are not my natural habitat—which honestly surprises me considering I grew up in the pre-Grindr era—but alas, cruising wasn't my forte. A waiter from the venue warned me that they were out there. I thanked him and asked if someone from the venue might escort me to the hotel, 200 yards away, across the parking lot. I was informed that they mightn't. Apparently, all those Tony Curtis gay undertones in the movie didn't inspire anybody in Shmedicine Shmat to their "I'm Spartacus!" solidarity moment.

So there I was, at midnight, calling Jer in Vancouver. He answered annoyed because he had to work in the morning. Yeah buddy, we've all got problems.

"Here's the address for the hotel I'm staying at," I said. *"This is the phone number to the local police station. If the phone goes dead or you hear anything, you have to call for help immediately."*

And then I ran. (I thought it best not to inform the rabidly repressed homophobes braying for my blood in the parking lot that I had my husband on the phone.) I ran from the venue to my hotel lobby like I had never run before because, reader? I had never run before. I want you to picture all 145 pounds of me,[1] at the time, "running" for my life. It wasn't pretty, but I made it, inhaler in hand. They chased me right up to the lobby, but my key got me in before they could follow, and I was safe.

---

1 Some would say closer to 300 pounds. But those people are homophobic.

That is, until I put the phone to my ear again … I think I might have been better off in the parking lot because my little Jer had turned into a Grizzly Baer.

SIDE BAER

I'm sorry, but I had never been more scared, mad, or worried in my life. I had to wake up at 5 a.m. for the breakfast shift at work and there I was, wondering if I'd still have a husband by the end of this phone call. So yes, I told him to pack his shit and cancel the tour and come home.

The next morning, I talked to the booker for the tour and explained that I would need security to safely continue the rest of the shows. Yes, the tour that was paying me [checks notes] one-hundred dollars a show, plus twenty for gas. I will forever be grateful for the supportive tone in which the owner of the chain of Canadian comedy clubs suggested to me that I might consider hiring my own security. With allies like that … it's worth remembering that technically Stalin was an Ally.

How did it come to this? How had Jeremy gone from scouting my comedy talent at our wedding to fielding midnight mob-violence-prevention phone calls and urging me to cancel lucrative tours with profit margins running into the ones and even tens of dollars? And what does any of this have to do with ADHD? Sorry, that last sentence was originally a margin note from my editor, but I decided to leave it in.

For many people with ADHD, life is a constant push and pull between creativity on the one hand, and devastating rejection on the other. In other words, having ADHD is a lot like being a comedian. Especially in Canada.

According to ADHD expert Dr. Edward Hallowell, MD, creativity is not just some la-di-da side effect of ADHD but is pretty critical to the whole thing. He notes that, "To thrive in life, people with ADHD need to create. So much so that I've come to regard this as a fundamental law in living a good life with ADHD." But that creative impulse isn't just straightforward good news since, "It can also tempt us to alter our internal reality through certain behaviors, such as casual sex or gambling or by means of substances like alcohol or other drugs." [Darcy coughs awkwardly. Slowly drops a glass pipe from his left hand. Slowly drops penis from right hand. I'm kidding—how could I have been typing if I were holding a pipe?]

One of the things I like about Dr. Hallowell is that for him, ADHD isn't a "disorder" (something bad) but a "trait" or "way of being" (something neutral, which comes with both advantages and disadvantages—again, like being Canadian). For every downside to ADHD, he identifies a twin upside. And this goes even deeper than his observation that "creativity is impulsivity gone right." (This one gem unearthed a bit of childhood trauma for me since when I asked my mom where babies came from, she told me "impulsivity gone wrong.")

Specifically, what I'm talking about is the fact that many neurodivergents experience something that has begun to be categorized by the experts as rejection-sensitive dysphoria or RSD. What it means is that many of us who have ADHD experience the discomfort from real or imagined criticism or rejection in a totally amplified, magnified way. See like right now, I'm worried that you don't think I explained that properly. YOU HATE ME, DON'T YOU?! Hallowell and his coauthor Dr. John J. Ratey call it an "exquisite sensitivity to criticism or rejection," which I'm really only able to handle because at least they think it's exquisite.

But wherever there's a downside there's an upside, right? And for Hallowell and Ratey, RSD is born with its much happier conjoined twin, RSE: recognition-sensitive euphoria. "As much as we can get down in the dumps over a minute criticism," they explain, "we can fly high and put to great use even small bits of encouragement or recognition."

To wit: I'm not sure everybody whose husband bought them a stand-up comedy class because their toast was funny at the wedding reception dinner would turn that into a twenty-year career in show business.

Now, we've touched on my hatred for classes and my history as a Second City drop-out, but for some reason this one was a bit different. Yes, it took place at a college; yes, I had to sit at a desk and listen to lectures. BUT there was a microphone, and I could walk up to it and make people laugh anytime I wanted? Without having to share the stage with anyone else?! What is this witchcraft?!

Oh, and there were hourly breaks. Can't recommend those enough. Yay for accessibility!

At the end of this grueling, three-hours-once-a-week, six-week-long class, we were allowed to show off our new expertise by performing at Zesty's restaurant on Commercial Drive in East Vancouver for a room full of our family and friends—provided they each paid ten dollars to attend with a minimum two drinks and a meal order. I was asked to close out the show. Did I get this headliner slot because I was the best? Yes. But it was also because the teacher knew I would go over my allotted time because—say it with me now—ADHDers have no sense of time.

I crushed with killer jokes like: "A lot of people are surprised to find out that I'm gay, but not as surprised as my first wife ... my second wife was just pissed off!" BOOM. Hello, *Tonight Show*! I can be there tomorrow.

As cheesy as the jokes are looking back on them now, I really did kill that night. And it was the greatest high I ever had (sorry, ecstasy). You see, not all addictions are drug or alcohol based; some are healthy, like being a stand-up comedian. Sorry, I couldn't type that one with a straight face, in any sense of the term.

The confidence I had that night after performing my killer set gave me something I had yet to have in life: a purpose. After that, I didn't want to become a stand-up comedian; I *was* a stand-up comedian. I borrowed my friend Bill's credit card (mine was maxed out, obviously; we already talked about ADHD money management with my dad, remember?) to do what every self-respecting comedian must do: buy a domain name. DarcyMichael.com was now mine. I was going to be a star, and internet fame was imminent. (Fourteen years away, to be precise.)

Incidentally, I should note that after fifteen years of Bill's credit card being charged for the domain's renewal, we finally transferred the payments over to my card and ... I immediately forgot to pay it, and now some random person in Italy owns it and wants ten thousand dollars to sell the domain name back to me. So might I suggest you visit darcyandjer.com for future updates on that unfolding story!

For those first few years, it was all RSE and no RSD. With the dedication that only someone with the mutant power of hyperfixation and a husband with a day job can muster, I poured myself into stand-up completely. Every night on the forty-five-minute drive home to Ladner from various spots around Vancouver, I would listen to recordings of my five-minute set over and over again—critiquing every joke, listening for the actual laughs from the audience, listening for where I could improve and where I could expand. This wasn't a job to me—it was an obsession.

An obsession that was starting to pay off. I was given the opportunity to audition for my own comedy special on the Comedy Network in Canada called *Comedy Now!*—at that point, with only two years' experience on stage, I couldn't help but think what you're probably thinking right now: Wow, they're a little late to the party, aren't they?

I booked it. It was official, I was going to be a household name in Canada, like "Shania Twain" or "kilometre," and the money would just roll right on in. I was paid $2,500 (Canadian!) for my life's work—twenty-two minutes of my greatest comedy ever written. This is a good point in the story to let you, the reader, know that I only had about eleven minutes of actually decent jokes at this time and was forced to double that in about a one-month period.

To film the special, I had to fly to Toronto, the cultural epicenter of the Greater Toronto Area. The day of the taping, I was told by the producers that I couldn't wear a hat on stage—INSERT GAY BALD MAN GASP HERE. Not gonna happen. As if I could go on stage in front of MILLIONS of potential viewers with my head exposed to the masses?! I refused to go on stage without it—I told them I would walk from this windfall of $2,500 unless someone with a flair for fashion understood my demands and backed me up.

We came to a compromise: I could, in fact, wear my page-boy cap, but I would have to wear it backward. Apologies to Samuel L. Jackson. Actually, I looked like Dom DeLuise and if you don't remember him, picture an Italian garden gnome with a backward page-boy cap. That was me.

We filmed it, and in typical Canadian TV fashion it sat on a shelf for two years. In that time, I'd like to think I was actually getting better at comedy. And then it aired to the masses and nothing changed. Did anyone watch? No idea. Did anyone review it? Nope. Did it change my career at all? No.

But eventually something had to, right?

The next few years were a creative wash, rinse, and repeat cycle. (As a bald man, I don't know why I hurt myself with these shampoo-based metaphors, but I guess I suffer for my art.) I did stage time, I wrote new jokes, I went on auditions, I made lifelong friendships with the funniest people in the world's funniest country, and I waited for a big opportunity.

And then my ship came in.

The good ship Oprah Winfrey.

Now, I know what you must be thinking. "I didn't know Oprah made Darcy famous! If that's true, shouldn't he be in the Trump cabinet right now?" But that's not exactly what happened.

Some of you will remember the launch of OWN, the Oprah Winfrey Network, which, coincidentally, was founded by Oprah Winfrey. In the lead-up to the launch, they needed an entire slate of TV shows to fill their schedule, and in that storm of opportunity, came an offer for me—me, Darcy Michael, who's living in government housing and working for one-hundred dollars a show in venues that will not accompany me past hate-filled throngs of post-show gorillas—to host a pilot.

I flew back to Ontario to start filming. The show was about unique families (I was from a unique family!) and so in theory, I would go and live with a family with a unique story and help over the course of time to tell their story and hopefully celebrate the impact they've made on their community. I believe the show had a super catchy name on the call sheet—it was something along the lines of *Untitled Oprah Project*—something that really grabbed people's attention.

I wish for the life of me I could remember the family's name, but let's be honest, remembering isn't my forte. Some would blame the ADHD, others would suspect my 4 p.m. post-Oprah doobies.

For privacy's sake, I will have to be a bit vague because I want to make sure that I'm not telling this family's story. Their story is not mine to tell. (Spoiler alert: CLEARLY OPRAH AGREED.)

I was in Toronto working with Corus entertainment on the pilot. I met with the family: lovely people who had immigrated to Canada to help protect their adult queer daughter from their home country where it was not safe to be, you know ... one of us.

The whole thing was very personal. At one point during the filming, I was sitting with the daughter in her bedroom talking about the sacrifices her parents made from living in their home country where they had wealth and prestige, then coming to Canada where these well-educated professionals were working as a cab driver and cashier. I sat in her room while she showed me pictures of friends who had been arrested and at times even killed back home for being queer ... the tears just flew out of my eyes. I remember crying so fast that the tears actually hit my glasses with a force, like I was a car trying to wash my windshield from the inside. I left the room for a few minutes just to gather myself, but of course the cameras followed me because ... I don't know, this was good TV? But I was just so touched and scared by her story.

We wrapped filming and I flew back home and waited ... and waited ... and waited.

I want you to imagine one day discovering in quick succession that 1) Oprah Winfrey knows who you are and 2) Oprah Winfrey doesn't like you.

I thought my ship had finally come in. But sometimes your ship runs aground on some jagged rocks. And sometimes those jagged rocks are THE FACT THAT OPRAH WINFREY WATCHED THE PILOT AND VERY SPECIFICALLY DIDN'T LIKE YOU.

Here comes that RSD, baby.

Now, here's the truth: I've been telling this story, to friends and to myself, for years. About how the woman who once meant so much to me that I built my whole dope-smoking schedule around her didn't like me and that it cost me a job.

But it wasn't until I sat down to write this that I went over these memories really carefully and in detail for the first time in years. And this time, I remembered something new.

I remembered a point at which I had to do a drive with the father of the family, just me and him in his car with some Go-Pros set up while I chatted with him about the sacrifices he'd made. And during that back and forth, there was a moment in this awkward conversation when he referred to his daughter's "issues," and he said something along the lines of, "If only we could fix her, it would be better …."

I remember very specifically that at that moment there was a fork in the road for me. (Not in the actual road; we were on Yonge Street in Toronto, which as I've already told you is the longest street in the world, DESPITE WHAT GUINNESS MAY SAY, hence no forks.)

But I remember thinking at that time that I could either let this comment go or I could push him to rephrase, be more supportive of the fact that his daughter doesn't have "issues" and that there was nothing about her to "fix."

And I just couldn't.

My brain was moving a million miles a minute. There I was with this opportunity to make good, confrontational, righteous TV. But I was also sitting with a father who has clearly already proven his unconditional love for his child by moving his entire family to a new country. A man trying to tell me his story, in a language that wasn't his, in a place that he was only just learning to live in. I've seen hatred and homophobia—they were waiting for me outside of that venue that night. This just wasn't that. I couldn't villainize this man by calling out his misunderstanding—because I knew that's all it was at this point. He'd either misspoken or misunderstood. So I let his comment slide, and we continued crawling along Yonge Street.

Looking back on it now (and I don't want to speculate), but perhaps it was that moment when the powers that be made the decision that I just didn't have it in me. I didn't have the instinct to go for broke, damn the consequences, for the sake of good television.

And if that's the case, not only is it true that, after all these years, I'm at peace with that decision, but I'm glad I made that choice—because I left that family feeling like we celebrated their evolving story. Their growth was what mattered to me, not the idea that I had to sensationalize or create drama or turmoil within their home. They were good people doing good things.

And even if that's not what cost me the gig? It's at least as credible a theory as every other idea I came up with for what I'd done to make Oprah hate me. (YOU'RE getting rejection-sensitive dysphoria! And YOU'RE getting rejection-sensitive dysphoria ...)

The fact is, a healthy dose of criticism and rejection comes along naturally with the creative expression that is part and parcel of life with ADHD. But when things start to get really painful is when we put that already-outsize creativity to work to explain why that friend hasn't returned our text message yet or what that coworker meant when they said that about our haircut.

My advice? (And by "my" I mean the advice I've gleaned from experts and friends and picked up along the hard slog of experience—through too many sleepless, anxious nights and tearful imaginary conversations with Oprah, always mediated by Gayle, to count.) In 99 percent of cases, you don't need to come up with your own theory about anything. Just be as good a friend/lover/son/daughter/coworker/actor/painter/comedian/acrobat/poet/surgeon/dancer/folk singer/etc. as you can be. Okay, maybe try to figure out what you're doing wrong if you're a surgeon. But otherwise, life comes with both dysphoria and euphoria.

Sometimes you kill, sometimes you need an escort home after the show. This ADHD life can be a real bitch, baby.

WHAT DOES THIS MEAN FOR YOU?

- The concepts of RSE and RSD can help to explain why an ADHDer might feel so elated and confident in themselves in one moment and completely defeated in the next. Beginning to recognize this pattern of behavior can be the first step toward finding deeper understanding and acceptance.

- The way that many ADHD brains are wired often goes hand in hand with an immense potential for creativity. "Outside the box" thinking and an ability to approach the world with a unique perspective can be a gift that may help you to connect with others and find incredible success.

CHOOSE YOUR OWN DISTRACTION

→ If you want to read about the first time I tried to take comedy classes and how I ended up just trying to learn gay cruising, turn to page 60.

→ If you want the story of my next big break that wasn't, and how to memorize lines for a sitcom when you have undiagnosed ADHD (hint: make up your own), turn to page 141.

→ If you want to learn how I almost fucked it all up, keep reading ...

8.
ADHD & PHYSICAL WELLNESS
MY FAT ACCOMPLI

Show business does funny things to the ego. If I audition for a role called "Fat Guy #3"—and yes, this is a real role that I have read for many times; and no, I have never been asked to audition for Fat Guy #1—and, hypothetically, I don't get the part (because I never do), what should be my take-away? Was I not fat enough? Was I too fat? Was the line reading bad? Was the line reading too good? Was the line reading too fat? Was it not fat enough?

In 2024, when stand-up comedy legend Jim Gaffigan lost fifty pounds using tirzepatide and released a comedy special called *The Skinny*, I couldn't be angry with him. Yes, it's true that twelve years earlier I had experienced very dramatic weight loss, and I had taped a show called *The Skinny*—but in my case, the producers hated it so much they buried the footage where no one could ever find it again. (And if you're thinking to yourself, "Oh, this is just Darcy's Rejection Sensitive Dysphoria from last chapter acting up again," ask yourself this question: have you ever seen *The Skinny with Darcy Michael*?)

And anyway, there were other differences between Jim's situation and mine. His *Skinny* was a stand-up special, mine was a talk show. He lost 50 pounds; I lost 120 pounds. He did it using subcutaneous injections of antidiabetic medication, I did it the old-fashioned way: wildly disordered eating and exercise bulimia. At last check, Gaffigan is still happily in his new, lean body. I, on the other hand, am very happy with my new fat one.

For context, when I was going through this weight-loss journey, I was still nearly a decade away from receiving my ADHD diagnosis. It's fairly well known that showbiz is a shitkicker when it comes to developing and sustaining not only a healthy body but also a healthy relationship with that body.

What is less well known is that ADHD, too, bears a very strong relationship to problem eating, certain extreme weight conditions, and gut health.

Well, buckle the fuck up, creeps, because this chapter has 'em all!

CHOOSE YOUR OWN TRAUMA!

A choice midchapter?! You're very welcome.

If you find weight or dieting talk triggering, might I suggest that you treat this chapter like it's breakfast and you're intermittent fasting and skip the fucker. The only difference is, you're not going to overcompensate by reading four chapters later.

Or continue on below ↓

First, the showbiz. Now, when you think showbiz, you think Canada. And when you think Canadian showbiz, there's only one city that always comes to mind: Calgary. Calgary is the kind of town that has built an entire identity around cowboys and oil, and somehow still doesn't realize it's gay. But way back in 2010 (eight years before my ADHD diagnosis), I was right in the heart of

Canada's closeted homoerotic city-petrostate to film a movie. And not just a movie, but a movie that featured some of the comedy talent I grew up watching like Harland Williams, Brian Posehn, and Mike Smith, who you will know better as Bubbles from *Trailer Park Boys* and who was also, oddly, at one point Axl Rose's guitar player … yes, this is the kind of random fact you get treated to when you buy a book written by a guy with ADHD who always has his Google tab open. The movie was called *Lloyd the Conqueror.* (You might not remember it because most of the awards it won were European.) I played the prestigious role of "Unicorn." It remains my belief that I had to play the unicorn because Calgary is so gay that if you go there already gay, they have to immediately upgrade you to superelite business-class ultra-gay so the oil bros can maintain plausible deniability. I was, physically, definitely still very much in my Fat Guy #3 phase. But since there was only one unicorn in the movie, my character required no numbers or adjectives.

Rather than enjoying this newfound freedom from/as a fat guy—instead of having fun working with some of my favorite comedians—the whole time we were filming I was feeling terribly sick. I was eating horribly, drinking lots every night after filming, and generally just feeling down. So down, in fact, that when filming wrapped, I did the smartest thing I could and went to Mexico with my best friend Momo for a week to an all-inclusive resort where I—brace yourself—ate horribly and drank too much.

Upon returning home to my loving husband, in a perpetual state of hungover awfulness, I realized that I was really not well. But I had never been a big drinker, so I assumed it was something to do with the booze. 'Cuz you know the old saying, "Tequila before beer, everything's cool; beer before tequila, blood in your stool." Honestly, do not tell me you've never heard that rhyme before—I've been having this argument for fifteen years straight with Jer and I'm not about to start up with you creeps!

Anyway, listen, I'm going to spare you the details here …

 **SIDE BAER**

Um, I think once blood in the stool has entered the chat, the spare-the-details train has left the station.

Babe, I'm writing, leave me alone.

God, I hate when he does that. What was I saying before Jer came along? Right, I needed someone to look at my butt. However, Grindr was still a few years out, and so there I was, sitting in an emergency room, doing the next best thing: cruising.

And just my luck, I found a doctor that loved my butt. (You can tell by if they wear their stethoscope hanging out of the back pocket.) In fact, this doctor loved my butt so much he wanted to look at it again and again, more and more profoundly, and all I could say was, "Here's hoping he finds Jer's watch!"

Well, he didn't find any timepieces. What he did find were some freaky looking polyps and now Jer and I were terrified because colon cancer runs in my family the same way that not running does.

What happened next really went against type for me as Fat Gay #1: I cut out wheat completely after the doctors diagnosed me as celiac, and, even more unlike me, I had a bunch of stuff taken out of my ass. Looking back now, this "cancer scare" was mercifully short and overdramatic. (Incidentally, two of the worst ways to have your genitals described.) I went out and did jokes about cancer—which are, today, the jokes I'm most ashamed of. I thought I'd earned the right to joke about cancer after what I'd been through. A very dear friend's experience would soon teach me that at that point, I hadn't earned shit.

For the record, here's a partial list of things I am allowed to make jokes about:

- ADHD
- The Dangers of Over-Planting
- Eyesight Loss (impermanent, weed-related)
- Gay Marriage
- Gluten Intolerance
- Straight Marriage (my parents are in one)
- Object Permanence
- Leisure Wear
- The Subtle Ambiguities of Ball Hairs vs. Beard Hairs
- Baby Carrots (What's the deal with them??! Where are their parents?!!!)

But after the drama of the polyp scare, and the radical shift of dropping gluten, I was suddenly ready for a new hyperfixation: "health" and weight loss. Of course, I didn't know it was a hyperfixation at the time—owing partially to the fact that I didn't know what hyperfixation was at the time. But I do now. You know that quote about how "every action produces an equal and opposite reaction"? I think it was Abraham Lincoln at the Getty Images Address? Anyway, I like to think of hyperfixation as the universe's equal and opposite reaction to ADHD—those of us who have trouble staying on task or following a particular line of thinking will also sometimes find ourselves completely locked in on a particular subject or activity with such intense focus that the rest of the world melts away. Don't believe me? I'll get 2009 Darcy to knit you a scarf.

And boy, was the new "healthy" weight-loss Darcy ever hyperfixated. Now, I say "health AND weight loss" as though they were two distinct ideas in my mind, but who am I kidding? You ever lose 120 pounds in six months? Well, with fanatical monomania and exercise bulimia, you, too, can almost lose it all!

CHOOSE YOUR OWN TRAUMA PART 2?!

I'm spoiling you all but really, I want to make sure you've been informed:

Listen, if food stuff's a motherfucker for you and you feel the need to skip ahead to the next chapter, I fully understand and support you on your journey. If you like, I can summarize quickly so you don't feel like you've missed anything when you rejoin the larger group: fatty went skinny badly and then came back to Fattyville as the mayor of loving yourself. Now turn to page 131.

Or continue on below. ↓

Actually, shit, maybe I should just end the chapter here and you can all move on to the next one? Ah, who am I kidding, I know how greedy some of you little creepers can be. I mean fuck, we've already done stool samples and colon polyps—we might as well go for broke.

I went nutso for what I thought was healthy. I didn't just start working out. Within a month of "eating healthy" and "working out," I was starting my day with a 12.5-mile (20K) bike ride, a 3-mile (5K) run, and a 1-mile (2K) swim. Almost every day. Then I would measure and weigh every piece of food going into my body.

And then I would weigh myself. Multiple times a day.

None of this was any better than how I was living before. I was just obsessed with food and exercise, to the point that I would be counting out almonds and putting them into little baggies to take on the road on tour with me. The little baggies I used to put weed in were now holding six almonds each and wowza, was I ever boring when I talked about any of it. I'd made it to skin and bones from potato skins and bongs in half a year. I had lost 120 pounds, and with it, any ability to be interesting at all.

But that didn't stop me from trying. I had landed my aforementioned talk show, *The Skinny with Darcy Michael*, to be filmed at the Winnipeg Comedy Festival. I interviewed guests like Alan Thicke; Caroline Rhea; and my good buddy Harland Williams, whose interview was so funny and bizarre I still can't think about it without crying-laughing.

This was it, I had done it. I'd lost weight and the industry was like, "Yes! He's skinny! That's what we've been waiting for! Give him all the money and accolades!"[1]

Then, in the midst of filming *The Skinny*, a TV director came to set one day and handed me three scripts for a multicam sitcom that they were hoping to get made with CTV, one of Canada's "big three" networks. In the script, he told me, was a gay character that was, at first, loosely inspired by me, and he'd love it if I would read the script and consider being a part of the show.

Well, you can imagine what I thought: Excuse me? I'm a talk show host! I'm the next Oprah (again)! I don't have time for your silly acting! I don't have time for a silly little sitcom that isn't even on the air!

And into the trash the scripts went. I was too busy hustling for the pre–Jim Gaffigan *Skinny*, and I simply didn't have time to worry

---

1 Money and accolades not included.

myself about a hypothetical sitcom. Spoiler alert, it wasn't ego that threw the scripts in the trash—it was ADHD. I was so consumed with my current project that the idea that something could come into my brain and interrupt that process was not permissible, so therefore the other project had to cease to exist in my brain. Nowadays, I have learned that compartmentalizing things can help me accomplish multiple projects at the same time without imploding.

And besides, I was about make my re-debut at the Just for Laughs festival in Montreal. Sure, they'd seen Darcy. But Darcy was dead. They were about to meet Skinny Darcy ...

I wrapped filming and a month later I was in Montreal—the sexiest city in the country. I'm not kidding, everyone there is so hot it's off-putting. AND NOW I WAS THERE AS ONE OF THEM. ONE OF US. ONE OF US. ONE OF US.[2] (Sorry, just had to put that in there because we were all thinking it.)

I stepped out onstage in front of the TV cameras and the country's most important stand-up comedy audience looking absolutely adorable in super skinny jeans, a dress shirt, and bow tie. And it's a good thing my outfit looked good, because there wasn't a joke to be seen for miles. I fucking tanked. My taping was a bomb. Skinny Darcy didn't bring any comedy with him; probably because his jeans didn't have any fucking pockets. This is what happens when you empty your weed baggies for almonds. Of course, that's not really true. There are gym-rat and yoga-fanatic and chia-seed-eating comedians who are every bit as funny as the clothing they wear for the activities they love. Comedians come in all shapes and sizes because comedy is human, and human beings come in all shapes and sizes.

---

2   Un de nous! Un de nous! Un de nous!

But Darcy Michael doesn't come in that size. And in order to pretend that I did, I had to force my body—and mind—into some pretty uncomfortable positions, including downward-facing dog among the world's most prolifically farting housewives in a hundred-degree Bikram studio. (Seriously, I was chewing air.)

Scientists are only now beginning to explore the connections between gut health and ADHD. I know this chapter has already had a lot of poop in it, but once more: a study of infant stool samples compared against ADHD diagnoses when the children were age ten found that the babies who grew up to have ADHD already had different gut bacteria than their neurotypical peers when they were six months old.[3]

But the relationship between eating, weight, and ADHD is already pretty well documented. Just over one fifth of candidates for bariatric surgery are estimated to have ADHD,[4] and this can make the follow-up measures to the surgery very difficult to follow through on.[5] In Australia, the medical weight management team at the Noi Clinic—okay, the name comes from the Greek term for a radical turnaround, *metanoia*, but I have to believe it's because they are also aware of how funny the world thinks it is when Australians say "no"—make ADHD assessment part of their work not only because of the huge overlap between ADHD and binge-eating disorder, but because the symptoms of ADHD seem almost naturally geared to make anybody's eating issues worse. As it turns out, a group of time-blind, dopamine-starved people with poor impulse control; difficulty planning ahead; executive dysfunction; a bunch of medication side effects; and a lifetime's worth of guilt, shame,

---

[3] https://www.everydayhealth.com/adhd/gut-health-and-adhd-is-there-a-link/

[4] https://digitalcommons.pcom.edu/cgi/viewcontent.cgi?article=1190&context=psychology_dissertations

[5] https://podcasts.apple.com/ca/podcast/australian-weight-loss-surgery-podcast/id1509598099?i=1000682544938

and stigma after being told they were stupid and/or lazy since they were children are sort of set up for trouble in the kitchen.[6]

It would take me a long time and, truthfully, gaining all the weight back again before I discovered the Healthy at Every Size movement. Healthy at Every Size is a lifestyle that encourages healthy eating and enjoyable physical activity as a way to feel better and live longer. (Now normally, we homosexuals don't like it when you call what we do a "lifestyle," but here I'll make an exception.) Unlike other programs, it does not believe weight loss through dieting is the way to become healthy.

I'm going to step out of the timeline of this chapter, and maybe even my charmingly sparkling persona, really quickly to just acknowledge that my food issues have never been "cured" and it's a constant struggle that I will continue to work on. That said, my ability to acknowledge that my body size doesn't define me has changed forever. As a gay man (showbiz, ADHD, and gay—what chance did I have?!), the pressure to look fit and be sexy was never ending. It's the only version of gay men I ever saw growing up and—even still—we idolize muscles and thinness. But my body isn't like that! So at some point, I had to step back and realize I was chasing this twink-body dream in a bear frame, and it just wasn't going to happen. Does that make me "less than"? No! I mean, quite literally, that was the problem! I weighed three to four times a twink body!

Honestly, I can't believe I just let a phrase go by where I said I was chasing a twink body and I didn't even make a joke. I hate these earnest parts of the book. But I can't help it if I've experienced personal growth. And that my personal growth also happened to include getting physically much bigger.

---

[6] See podcast in footnoote 5 and https://www.noiclinic.com.au/adhd

I really don't know when or how it happened, but there came a moment when I was walking around our house shirtless in a pair of booty shorts and a shawl when someone knocked on the front door ... and I just opened it to talk to them. There was no hesitation, there was no running around to throw on a baggy sweater to cover myself up. I just stood there, looking like the gay garden gnome I was meant to be. I found myself understanding that no one actually cares that I'm topless at a beach—and if they do care, that's on them, not me. Plus let's be honest, if I cared about what I looked like, I'd probably start with hair-plugs.

The takeaway here is that ADHD can be a cruel bitch on your brain and body. Remembering to eat and drink water during the day when I'm hyperfixating on plants or comedy or whatever other hobby I've picked up that week to give me dopamine is hard. But now I've learned that when I finally realize I'm hungry, I'M HUNGRY RIGHT NOW and all the food in the world won't actually satisfy me. So I started with simple things like setting food and water alarms on my phone. Then I started noting that I'm a mindless eater when I watch TV or movies, so now I doom scroll on my phone instead while I watch. FUN!

Please note that was sarcastic. But also, very true.

The point is, eventually, when my big break finally did come (spoiler alert: I got famous with my husband on a massive Chinese government spying-and-breakdancing app. Apologies if you bought this book because of *Lloyd the Conqueror*), I was big for it. And I don't think that's an accident.

But back in 2012, when I was the first weight-loss comedian to tape a show called *The Skinny*, I was a long way off from that big break. My talk show was in digital mothballs. My skinny return to Montreal was a bomb. My return to the stage and screen was a bust.

And then an email came in from that sitcom director ... was there any chance I'd be interested in auditioning for that role he mentioned?

Fuck me, where are those scripts?!

WHAT DOES THIS MEAN FOR YOU?

- A sudden change in your health, or a loved one's health, can trigger all kinds of responses, especially if you're a neurodivergent thinker. It's incredibly common for a new diagnosis to elicit a feeling of lack of control that can allow for the hyperactive part of your brain to take over. Seek guidance and help from professionals and try to remember to use the tools that have gotten you this far.

- Hyperfixation is an extremely common byproduct of ADHD processing. It can come in the form of constantly comparing one situation to another, replaying a social interaction in your mind over and over, or making the same thing for lunch every day until you can't eat it anymore. The key to overcoming a cycle of hyperfixation is to try to recognize when it's happening, so you can get at the root cause.

CHOOSE YOUR OWN DISTRACTION

→ If you want to read how I first got into comedy, turn to page 105.

→ If you want to see me try to develop my own sitcom, turn to page 29.

→ If you want to know how the audition went, keep reading ...

9.
ADHD & MONEY
A DEFICIT?!
IN THIS ATTENTION ECONOMY?

Can I be honest for a second? At this point in my life, even though it was secretly in charge of everything I was doing and the way I was doing it, I didn't know a thing about ADHD. The only attention deficit that mattered to me was the deficit between how hard I was hustling and how little anyone was paying attention.

Yes, I auditioned for the role. I filmed a first audition at home. Then I filmed a callback audition, still in Ladner. Then, "Holy shit, CTV wants to fly me to Toronto to do a chemistry test?" Hey, I failed Earth Science but fuck it, I'm in! I flew to Toronto and spent a whole day being paired up in front of the cameras with potential co-stars for the role of a lifetime! A funny, gay role inspired by funny, gay me!

And then ... I didn't get the part.

GODDAMNIT, HOW MANY PEOPLE'S PHONE NUMBERS DOES OPRAH WINFREY HAVE?!?!

The heartbreak was real. In just a few short months I'd gone from having all the momentum I'd been waiting for to ... nothing. In the summertime, the sitcom couldn't even get my attention. Now it was rejecting me with all the gusto of a grinning guest on a "You Dumped Me But Look At Me Now" episode of Ricki Lake.

If it hadn't been for Jer, we'd have been flat broke. By which I mean, we were broke, but at least his corporate ass was covering the rent while I was flailing and failing. In the time that I'd been graduating from fat pothead to skinny almond fiend, Jer had actually graduated—like from a school!—and had left his restaurant job to start his new life as a corporate stooge. Financially speaking, we were never more grateful to have his steady, dependable Bert energy to counterbalance my mercurial, neurodiverse Ernie. Because careerwise, at this point, Ernie was living in Oscar's trash can. Have you ever been rejected for a role that was based on you? I wouldn't recommend it. It will make you long for the days of losing out on Fat Guy #3.

But the year had one final indignity in store for me. It was just before Christmas, and my agents got a call about a small role in the pilot of the sitcom. It wasn't a gay lead; it was the office weirdo. Think the guy that pops in with some non sequiturs at the end of a scene and then leaves. The role was just for the pilot, which filmed in two weeks' time in Toronto. Who knows, if the show got picked up, maybe the character might show up again once or twice during the season.

Did I want the part?

Did I want the part? Did they forget they were talking to the guy who'd thrown their script in the garbage when they were offering him a lead?! Now, after passing me over for a gay role inspired by me in favor of some straight actor, they wanted to placate me with some eunuch day-player part that I would film in Toronto in January?

Yes, I wanted the part.

One of the main reasons I could mentally justify this to myself, aside from my longstanding attachments to food and shelter, was because the show starred one of my favorite comedians (and soon to become one of my favorite people), Dave Foley from *The Kids in the Hall* and *NewsRadio*. There are three groups of people for whom members of the Kids in the Hall sketch troupe are basically minor deities—Canadians, queers, and Gen-Xers—and as a dick-loving fella born in Ontario in 1980, I just barely make the trifecta. I also happen to think that the pilot for *NewsRadio* is hands down one of the best multicam pilots ever made—and yeah, I betcha didn't predict that this book would contain any Joe Rogan endorsements, didja? (For clarity's sake, that last sentence was very much a joke, I do not endorse Joe Rogan doing anything besides perhaps turning his microphone off.)

We filmed our pilot, for *Spun Out*, in front of a live studio audience and instantly I was hooked. Addicted. Acting in front of a studio audience is just like stand-up only better, because it pays real money AND the audience is forced to laugh. The dream! Also, there are surprisingly few parking lots full of violent rural homophobes lying in wait! Double dream!

Spun Out was set in a public relations business—hence the "spin." (I guess the gay character was the "out"?) Dave played the company's owner, and my character, a lowly office drone with never-defined duties at the firm, was named Gordon. In retrospect, this was actually a pretty good sign. American readers probably can't fully appreciate the gravitas and honor carried by the name "Gordon" in English-speaking Canada, and I don't think there's any equivalent in the USA. I don't really know whether the best way for me to communicate how important a name it is up here is to tell you that the first full-length album by one of the country's biggest-ever bands, the Barenaked Ladies, was called *Gordon* and went platinum, or that that the country's most important political newsmagazine, *Maclean's*, once ran a piece simply headlined

"11 Famous Canadian Gordons."[1] And you know every Gordon counts if they won't round it off to a top ten. Two of Canada's greatest departed musical legends, Gordon Lightfoot and Gord Downie, wore the name, and Jer tells me that Gordie Howe was a really big deal in hockey, but I think he's just trying to sound butch.

Well, a little of that ol' Canadian Gordon magic must have rubbed off on me, because shortly after we filmed the pilot, the series got picked up, and instead of returning for one or two appearances, I was added to the regular cast.

There was just one note—the director of the series felt that Gordon had been a little bit too svelte in the pilot. Was there any chance I would consider putting back on a few pounds, for the sake of the comedy?

It was a totally inappropriate request, an invasion of privacy, and reduced my own body, that most sacred extension of my very self, to a mere prop. If I hadn't already started gaining the weight back several weeks earlier, I would have given that guy such a piece of my mind!

But all I could think of was that my losing streak was over! Was this the kind of classic all-or-nothing thinking anecdotally associated with ADHD and, according to mental health journalist Saya Des Marais, regularly associated with frequent ADHD comorbidities like depression and OCD?[2] Well, sure! But all-or-nothing's only a problem on the nothing side, right? This was all, baby! And mama loves all!

Now listen, I know that by writing a book, I'm opening myself up to the possibility of nasty reviews. That's inevitable. But a couple

---

1 https://macleans.ca/society/life/11-famous-canadian-gordons/

2 https://www.rula.com/blog/adhd-black-white-thinking/

that I feel helpless to prevent are, "I thought it got really repetitive how members of The Kids in the Hall kept intervening with life-saving advice. Also the author's penis was simply too large for me to enjoy the writing."

I'm sorry, but those are two criticisms that I just can't do anything about! If multiple Kids in the Hall saved my well-endowed life at key moments in time, that's just the way that it was!

In this case, it was Dave Foley who took me under his wing (figuratively, not literally; it was Mark McKinney who played the Chicken Lady) and helped prevent what otherwise would have been the most likely ADHD catastrophe to befall my TV-star turn: bad money management.

Even the squarest of straitlaced neurotypicals find it hard to go from busted to flush without going a little crazy on the retail therapy. But an ADHDer leaping over full tax brackets in a single bound is a recipe for disaster. When it comes to ADHD and money management, there are certain huge pitfalls.

Fine Print: I prefer to call it Fine! Print, because this is the kind of minute detail that makes those of us with ADHD throw up our hands and say "Fine!" in surrender rather than working through on our own. This is how a lot of us get into financial agreements that aren't nearly as good as we think they are, and why I'm still getting a CD from Columbia House every month even though the only thing I can use them for is deflecting crows from fig trees.

Dopamine Deals: Those of us with ADHD are constantly on the prowl for hits of dopamine (one way or another, I'm always looking for D), and the fact is, there's almost no faster way to a quick shot of the good stuff than good ol' buying stuff. Spending feels good! Now that said, let me be clear—if you're reading this passage in a bookstore or an airport, thinking about whether or not this book is for you, it's important not to be fanatical about these things.

Tomorrow Never Comes: That came out a lot more depressed-German-existentialist than I meant it to. But famously, as Dr. Hallowell will tell you, those with ADHD live in only two timeframes: Now and Not-Now. The medium- and long-term financial consequences of our decisions are quite literally inconceivable. Trying to explain compound interest to me is like trying to explain the multiverse theory to a chamois.

Between challenges with planning, impulse control, executive function, and time blindness, most people with ADHD are sitting ducks when they're lucky enough to have a big influx of cash.

And that's where, if you're lucky, you turn to Dave Foley. (I don't mean that literally, obviously—not everyone will have the support of a Kids in the Hall veteran. Feel free to turn to a prominent sketch comedian and sitcom veteran from your own national tradition, a Tina Fey or John Cleese. Maybe not John Cleese.)

One day at lunch break I asked Dave, who at this point had been steadily working for years in the industry—what the one piece of advice was that he had for me starting out. *"Don't spend the money,"* he said, going against every impulse exploding inside of me. *"Pay off your debts and nothing else for the first season. Second season, maybe buy yourself something nice and small but save it. If we get a third season, then go be stupid."*

This simple, straightforward advice would prove to be extremely valuable. Like I said, it helped me dodge my biggest ADHD-bomb on the sitcom. But it couldn't save me from all of them.

Filming the first season of *Spun Out* was some of the most fun I'd ever had. (Narrator foreshadowing voice: Perhaps it was ... too much fun?) I made lifelong friendships with castmates like Rebecca Dalton and producer Andrew Barnsley, who I'm still working with today. I was paying my bills, and thanks to Dave, even when it was all over, I didn't have a Range Rover lease to pay. In fact, all I had was no debt, good credit, and a good credit on my resume.

But ADHD is a sneaky li'l bitch. It's a whirring, whizzing whack-a-mole in the mental Chuck E. Cheese of the mind. I'd brought the foam mallet down hard on financial mismanagement. But memory struggles, rejection-sensitive dysphoria, and object permanence were popping up unscathed. These are three different phenomena, but they're also related, so think of them kind of like Wilson Phillips? We'll get to all three, just "Hold On."

For starters, memory struggles: I couldn't memorize my fucking lines! Clinical psychologist Sharon Saline has written about ways that executive dysfunction and, believe it or not, emotional regulation—YEAH, I FUCKING KNOW OKAY?!—combine to make the working memory of those with ADHD seriously "uneven."[3]

In stand-up, I had always used a jokebook that I brought up with me onstage and left on the stool while I performed. I made it part of the act, going back and "making notes" on how jokes went, but when I look back now, I know that this was an early ADHD coping adaptation before I even knew it. But now, in front of a live studio audience and for much bigger paychecks, I didn't have a notebook. But I didn't miraculously have a better memory, either.

One way that I coped was to make up lines. Gordon's lines were usually "buttons," meaning that they came at the end of the scene, as a punchline, and nobody else was dependent on me to get their own lines right. So then I'd make up a line for Gordon, which, according to the studio audiences, was usually funnier than what was in the script. Ultimately, this became part of our working model for Gordon: I would read the scripted line, then rattle off five or six impromptu gags.

---

3   https://www.psychologytoday.com/ca/blog/on-your-way-with-adhd/202402/understanding-adhd-working-memory-challenges

But first, I still had to read the written line. The solution arrived at was as embarrassing as it was ingenious: since the show took place in an office full of desks (remember those? LOL), and everyone's desk had a computer on it, why couldn't Gordon's computer actually be a functioning computer, really connected to the internet, so I could have my script open on it?

A more confident, more experienced, more neurotypical performer might have laughed off the arrangement. I might even have gotten cocky about it, considering that I must have been pretty good at what I was doing if they were willing to make accommodations as unconventional as these.

But that's not how RSD works! In their book *ADHD 2.0*, Dr. Edward Hallowell and Dr. John Ratey describe RSD as the "tendency on the part of people who have ADHD to overreact precipitously and disastrously to even the slightest perceived put-down, dis, or vaguely negative remark." These doctors also make the case that RSD is counterbalanced by its opposite, something they call "RSE"; "recognition-sensitive euphoria."[4] Anybody who's ever seen me onstage mainlining the spotlight would know that these guys are onto something with that one. But that wasn't happening while we were filming *Spun Out*. Instead, week after week—even as it got objectively less and less likely the further we got in—I was convinced that they were going to fire me. If I had known what hyperfixation meant back then, I would have been able to see the signs that I wasn't allowing myself to live in the moment and enjoy this wild ride of making a sitcom. Instead, I was obsessed and fixated with the fear that I was going to get fired at any moment. The impostor syndrome set in so hard I wouldn't feel anything like it again until later on, when somebody paid me to write a book.[5]

---

4   *ADHD 2.0*, page 11.

5   Please turn your attention to my author photo.
PEOPLE WHO AREN'T AUTHORS DON'T HAVE AUTHOR PHOTOS!!!

How did I deal with it all? I drank a lot of booze, and I leaned into the hyperfixation. There are scenes I don't even remember filming. Another scene involved riding a tandem bicycle across the set with another actor, and I was so sauced that we careened into the walls of the office, which I will remind you, being a TV set, was not really a wall and not really an office. It wasn't very responsible, but in my defense, the statistics for on-set Canadian drunk-driving tandem-bicycle accidents are inconclusive at best.

But my biggest ADHD fuck-up had to do with object permanence. Object permanence is one of the first faculties that a baby develops as they're becoming a toddler (it's why peekaboo! works; it's also why they rarely show proper gratitude for that Christmas present you carefully picked out), whereby a person is able to retain consciousness of something, or someone, when they are not physically present or immediately visible. This ability is something that people with ADHD struggle with a lot. Out of sight really can mean out of mind for us, unless we're extremely mindful and take special steps to correct it.

I was in Toronto for three months soaking up booze and celebrity advice and live audience accolades. My husband and our daughter were on the other side of the second biggest country in the world.

So Jeremy sent me an email.

WHAT DOES THIS MEAN FOR YOU?

- Between challenges with planning, impulse control, executive function, and time blindness, most people with ADHD are sitting ducks when they're lucky enough to have a big influx of cash. All I can recommend is the Dave Foley method of money management: don't spend it all on something stupid. My new rule has become 10 percent: I can spend 10 percent of a paycheck on something silly, the rest has to go toward things like mortgage and house maintenance. But I should clarify that house maintenance is plants. See the sneaky workaround? Shhh, don't tell Jer.

- ADHD and neurodivergent processing can impact your work-life balance in many ways. Concepts like object permanence and RSD can make it extremely challenging to remain on-task and focused. Remember to step back and ask yourself for the facts—has someone actually said you're going to get fired? No? Then perhaps RSD is tricking you into a spiral that shouldn't exist. Ask yourself for the facts, write them down, and don't let yourself spiral for the sake of it, because you could be missing out on just enjoying yourself.

CHOOSE YOUR OWN DISTRACTION

→ If you want to read about the first time I met Grace, turn to page 90.

→ If you want to learn why you've never heard of *Spun Out,* turn to page 141.

→ OH, WHO THE FUCK ARE WE KIDDING, if you want to know what Jer said, keep reading ...

10.
ADHD & WHAT'S IN FRONT OF YOU

HAS ANYONE SEEN MY OBJECT PERMANENCE? I SWEAR I JUST HAD IT!

Okay, before we go any further, I think we need to take a second to acknowledge what we're doing and maybe pat ourselves on the back so fucking hard we dislodge that bit of falafel from lunch.

For real, though. Look at us. A couple of regular Distracted Denises and we're getting through a goddamn book together. You're reading a book. I'm writing a fucking book! For most of us, this is absolutely not what comes easiest, and so we have every reason to be proud. Feel how many pages you've got in your left hand! (Don't feel bad if you just jumped straight here on a Choose Your Own Distraction, that was totally legit! Also, obviously, don't feel bad if you're reading a Japanese or Hebrew or other translation of this book into a language read from right to left. Just feel how many pages you've got in your right hand instead! And hey, I haven't forgotten about you audiobook people, either—look how far away you are now from your house!)

Books aren't always easy for ADHDers, but they're able to do things other artistic forms just can't accomplish. For instance, take bio-pics. In those movies, the main character is only ever on the way straight up like a rocket ship or plummeting to earth like an Elon Musk rocket ship. But in my experience, that's not what life is actually like.

Take this period in my life. Was this a rock-and-roll-will-never-die-man, I'm-gonna-write-my-name-across-the-world-Ma part of the story? Or are these more like bloated-in-aviator-sunglasses-buying-cocaine-wearing-a-white-suit scenes? Put it this way: if this were a movie montage, would they be playing "Machine Gun" by The Commodores or "Free Bird" by Lynyrd Skynyrd? (If you don't know those two songs off the top of your head, I'll wait here while you go listen to them both on your phone and realize that one or the other, sometimes both, have been used every single time you've ever seen a movie where this stuff happens.)

But the fact is, this particular part of my life was nothing if not ambiguous. That's one of the things I love about Dr. Hallowell's approach to ADHD: he doesn't see it as purely a disorder, and he doesn't see it as a gift brought in by kind pixies while you slept, either. He views it as a particular set of wiring that has some super shitty aspects, along with some really good shit.

I don't think that's just how ADHD is—that's how life is! And it's certainly where things were at as I was filming the first season of *Spun Out*.

Ambiguity, the good with the bad. Shortly after filming wrapped on season one, I went on to win a spot in the NBC *Stand-Up for Diversity* showcase (good!). I lost in the finals (bad!), but still somehow managed to land a headline tour of U.S. colleges. Good? Sure, but maybe better if it hadn't been a bunch of Evangelical colleges.

I was at a Christian college in Ohio and there were all of six people in the audience about ten minutes before my hour-long set. That's literally half the number of disciples, as these students would have well known—or maybe they hadn't taken that class yet, I don't know. I told the bookers in charge of the show that if we had a minimum audience of ten folks at showtime, I would go on. My embarrassment at my lack of drawing power was slightly balanced out by my excitement for a night off, or "Sabbath." Two minutes before the show started, there were nine people in the crowd. But luckily for me, I had brought my friend Kat with me! So, how fun, now there were ten.

My first joke was about being gay. Suddenly, there were six people in the audience.

YAY for diversity!

Slightly more encouragingly, during our hiatus from filming season one, I entered into a development deal with the broadcaster, CTV, to develop my own sitcom. And as *Spun Out* got picked up for a second season, I managed to negotiate a 150 percent pay raise, given all the impromptu joke-writing I was doing on set. As a vote of confidence, the network told us that the season-two premiere would air right after the Super Bowl. Holy shit, I thought, we're going to be on the air for years!

A quick note for British, American, and Australian readers currently wondering if *Spun Out* was some massive, multiseason Canadian hit you've never heard about: it was not. In fact, we got canceled after two seasons. Why? Well, I don't want to get into the salacious details because I'm not one to gossip, but if I were one to gossip, I'd say pull up a comfy seat for this next sentence: A week before we were to make our big Super Bowl debut, one of my castmates was arrested for voyeurism when a hidden camera was found by his young female tenants. Sorry, I just had to go Purell my hands after typing that sentence. No, it wasn't Dave Foley, and no, I don't actually know the outcome of the case because it was such a moment that I can't even begin to explain. My friend and our producer, Andrew Barnsley—who would go on to make *Schitt's Creek* and find deserved success as an amazing TV producer who never cast me again—called me to tell me the news and I was floored. I was so upset for these poor tenants, I didn't even begin to think about the implications for our show. But the network did! CTV canceled the Super Bowl plans and then buried our second season in the dead zone of summer, never to be mentioned again. It's funny, because no one even told us it was canceled. To this day, I've never been told it was canceled. They just sold the wardrobe and sets and that was it.

But before season two could be shitcanned, first we had to make it! For the second season, we lost our live audience, which meant we lost a lot of the joy that had come with making the show, at least for me. But it was still three months of hard, boozy work in Canada's biggest and most important city (besides Calgary).

And that's where the object permanence comes in.

Remember three weeks ago, when I told you to put the book down to look up those two songs? And then you started checking iMDB to see if you could find out what movies they were used in? And then you googled to see if Robin Wright and Sean Penn were still married, or even married yet, when she made *Forrest Gump*? And then you tried to find out why Sean Penn had given an Oscar statue to Volodymyr Zelenskyy? And then you didn't think about this book for just over twenty days until you saw it under your laptop charger and thought, "Hey! I was liking that book!" and started reading it again? That's how difficulty with object permanence goes. And confession time: that's how I am even with the people in my life ... sometimes including Jer.

Today, I keep photos of my friends and loved ones all around me because, well ... because of this next part of the story. Because at this period, when my wildest ambitions felt at their absolute closest, but still just out of reach—when I was spinning my wheels in undiagnosed ADHD and disordered eating and exercise bulimia—I made the love of my life feel like I wasn't really there. And I wasn't.

SIDE BAER

Ahem. So I wrote Darcy this email …

JEREMY! Quit interrupting and distracting me, we'll get to that part in a minute. First, I need to back up a moment. It's not a true ADHD story if we don't have timeline jumps, subject switches, and all that other shit.

Listen, I know we've already talked about hyperfixation a lot in this book; so much so that you could say at this point I'm a bit obsessed with the idea. In fact, you might go so far as to say I'm hyperfixating on hyperfixation. And you would be correct, but there's a reason I'm bringing it up again: hyperfixation and object permanence go hand in hand. And hyperfixation isn't always about hobbies or a new TV show—a lot of us experience hyperfixation with people.

This can be true in both platonic and romantic relationships, but obviously things can get a lot more fraught when it comes to Door Number Two in that scenario. If you google the terms "ADHD" and "love bombing"—don't do it now, I can't afford to lose you for another three weeks!—you'll find out that there is a whole thing online where ADHD hyperfixation plays out in crushes and new relationships in a way that gets confused with a particular style of emotional manipulation in which one partner simply overwhelms the other with attention and over-the-top displays of affection (sometimes followed by just as suddenly running cold).

Anyway, I tell you all this because I had made a new friend—we'll call him Todd 'cuz that's what the legal department told me I could get away with when changing his name. I love Todd, he is a great person. But unfortunately for Todd, he rather quickly became my hyperfixation. And in turn, made my object permanence even worse.

Now I know you creeps all want salacious details but here's the simple truth: no, it wasn't an affair; no, it wasn't anything untoward. It was, simply put, a close friendship that was shiny, new, and exciting. And as I chased the dopamine that I found with my pal, I found myself slipping further into object permanence struggles. On top of this, I was living in Toronto for three months to film *Spun Out* and the rest of the time I was touring with my stand-up act—and Jer, being the saint that he is, was back home wondering whether I was going to at least call or text—he probably would have even settled for a midnight-emergency-small-town-gay-bash-evasion-tactic like old times—because I hadn't been.

Until one day I opened my email, and lo and behold, there it was. An email from my husband—one that I won't share, because boundaries are important, but that I will recap quickly:

> Hey Asshole,
>
> Remember us, your husband and daughter?! We exist and currently we're existing without you and that's not fair. I love you and I want you to chase your dreams, but I also need you. Please come home soon, because if not, I'm not sure there will be a home for you.
>
> Go fuck yourself,
> Jer

SIDE BAER

So that's not even remotely what the email said. But ... yes, I felt like while my husband was losing weight and gaining friends and fame, I was losing him. And I needed to know if that was the case, because I was done waiting. I wanted him to be my husband.

Hi, it's me Darcy; I'm back, sorry about our little interrupter there. And about my allergies.

He was not losing me. His email dropped my heart ten stories underground. I was devastated. Nothing I did was out of malice, and in fact, until a few years later when I would learn about my ADHD and object permanence, I had no way to even explain how any of this was happening.

To say that I ran home is actually an understatement. On the spot, I canceled a weekend of headline shows in Ottawa, drove from there to Peterborough to get my things, and caught the next flight home. I was in a full-on panic. I was terrified of losing the two people who I wanted to share everything with. Don't tell him I said this, but I'm so fucking grateful he sent that message.

SIDE BAER

Pop quiz for my stoner husband! Who did you literally just ask to check this chapter for typos?

Jer's email opened up a line of communication between us that had never existed before—a line of communication that has continued to be so clear and honest and real that at times it can be quite difficult. But I've learned that I need to hear my partner's fears and do everything I can not only put those flames out with words but with actions.

I learned to text or call Jer every day that I was on the road—not always for my sake but for his. I had never really thought about the fact that while I was busy touring or filming and was surrounded by all these people, half of Jer's life had left him. There was no one taking up that space for him. We put our heads together to figure out how much time we're mutually comfortable with being apart. It's ten days. We learned that after ten days, we both start to go spinny.

I also learned that I needed things like photos of my family in my office, and that when I was on the road, something as simple as opening my suitcase and seeing a picture of Jer and Grace would remind me of home.

It was good. It was actually really good. But I don't think either of us fully realized how much that email had changed things. From that point, a process started. A slow but undeniable, dawning realization that what I was really after might not actually be out there at all.

But that was still a way to go.

WHAT DOES THIS MEAN FOR YOU?

Hyperfocusing on what's in front of you at any given moment—and tuning everything else out—is a common occurrence for folks with ADHD. Setting breaks to check in with yourself or a loved one regularly can be a small but very effective tactic to keep you grounded.

CHOOSE YOUR OWN DISTRACTION

→ If you want to read about me and Jer's first date, turn to page 79.

→ If you have no self-control and want to jump straight to the happy ending, turn to page 208.

→ If you want to read about my biggest, most life-changing break (an ADHD diagnosis), keep reading ...

11.
ADHD & YOUR DIAGNOSIS

YOU CAN'T SPELL "DIAGNOSIS" WITHOUT "KNOW." WELL, ACTUALLY YOU CAN.

As a gay man, I am automatically indebted for life to the vast richness of Greek culture. For starters, the Greeks invented olive bowls, and anal, and lesbians—our natural allies. (And, to judge from the turnout at our live shows, the people who keep the electricity on at my and Jer's house.) But beyond loose-fitting sheetwear and erotic poetry, the Greeks also gave us George Michael and much of the English language.

The English word "diagnosis" comes from Greek, with a little detour through Latin, which is like, "Oh, I'm sorry, could this linguistic situation be any more Mediterranean and therefore hotter?" *Dia-* basically means "apart or separate," and *-gnosis* means "knowing." And while I don't think this is what they had in mind, I think maybe it does explain how sometimes a diagnosis comes into your life, and now you know something that separates you forever from the time before you knew.

How do you know you're in trouble? And how do you know when you're getting out of it? For many neurodiverse people, the diagnosis—the official announcement of a problem—is ironically exactly the moment when things start to turn around. And as you know, my "diagnosis" came from an unexpected place. (If you're just joining us here because you skipped ahead or because you're pooping at a friend's and they left this book on the back of the toilet, it came from sketch comedy legend Bruce McCulloch, see page 34.)

But also, sometimes things can only start getting better after they've hit rock bottom, and this is only a cliché if you also consider, I don't know, "gravity" and the "second law of thermodynamics" to be clichés. So before we talk about my diagnosis, I think it might help to talk about rock bottom for a moment.

After *Spun Out* got canceled, I didn't know what my next steps were going to be, workwise or moneywise. On Dave Foley's financial advice, we hadn't let Jer quit his job, and Jer will be the first one to tell you that we were so grateful for that advice. We were now finally debt-free. But we were still renting our little apartment with dreams of buying a house one day, and now those dreams were looking further and further out of our reach.

So I was without work and had no real plan, but I was in desperate need of a dopamine hit. I therefore decided we were ready to expand our family a bit when I saw a post about a basset hound who needed rescuing. The hound's name was Sally, which we extended to Sally Field, which is cute, until we get to all the rest of the parts of this story, and it just becomes kind of awkward. Sally Field had been badly abused. (See, even that phrase; it's ... not good.) She had major resource-guarding issues related to anything that she deemed hers, and at times this extended beyond food and toys and dog treats to things like the hoodie our daughter Grace was wearing or a duvet that someone was dragging down the hall. It very soon became apparent that we were in way over our heads.

Nothing is worse than a basset hound with a ferocious temper, because everyone wants to get right into a basset hound's face because they're so fucking adorable. At one point, there I was, standing holding a stick that Sally had decided was hers and wouldn't you know it, there's her jaw locked onto my inner thigh ready to rip my arteries open. And I couldn't help but think, *hmmm, maybe this wasn't the greatest idea.*

Sally Field attacked Jer (okay, maybe that time the name sounded a little funny) and Grace so much that I had to cancel a stand-up tour to stay home to work with a team of vets and trainers, and all the while I was constantly covered in bites from her. It was torture. For a while, Jer and I would make excuses for the dog—"She only bit me because I hadn't realized that the steak I was eating was actually hers," or "Really, it was my fault that I put on a shoe she wanted, so in some ways I deserved to almost lose that toe,"—but they only highlighted the situation for what it was: beyond repair.

The nightmare day came when she nearly mauled a child, and we had to make the brutally hard decision to have her put down. I had never felt pain like that before, and as timing would have it, the day we said goodbye to Sally Field (ugh, I'm sorry Actual Sally Field—this was so much cuter with Paul Anka on Gilmore Girls) was the day I was heading into Vancouver to record my stand-up album *Family Highs*.

I thought I was at rock bottom. This had to be rock bottom, right? I was without work, my dog was dead, and I had to go pretend to be funny on stage for an album recording that I couldn't afford to reschedule.

Two days later, one of my best friends in the world, Ashley, was diagnosed with cancer. And this? This is why I don't get to make cancer jokes after some silly polyps. This is why I didn't actually know cancer for shit.

So now. Now's the bottom. Right?

Time for a distraction.

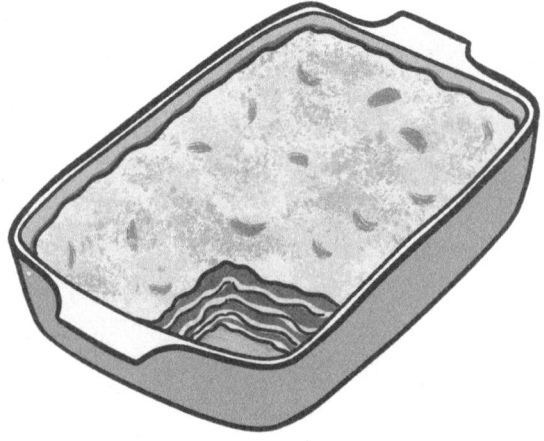

GLUTEN-FREE LASAGNA

Okay, you know what—we've gotten through a lot of this book so far. And while I know it's a lot for you—think of me! I had to write all this shit out, and then I still had to read it! And let me tell you something: it's not even easy when it's about the good stuff! So just imagine how it feels when I'm telling you about one of my most cherished friends being sick—ah, fuck! It's starting again!

My point is, I think we deserve a little break. A nice little palette cleanser, like a sorbet, or more specifically a lasagna. Sometimes, it just feels good knowing there's cheese in your future, so let's take a break from all this drama and have a little snack. And by little, I mean it usually weighs about five pounds by the time it's ready.

Ingredients

1 tablespoon olive oil (Greek, if possible, to pay it forward)

Something white, with layers, that'll make you cry ... but since I can't always be there, get an onion (a medium-size one, diced)

3 garlic cloves, minced

1 pound (450g) ground meat or meat substitute (This can be anything you want. Well, for most readers—I'm looking at you Armie Hammer.)

1 teaspoon salt, divided

1 teaspoon black pepper, divided

1 (28-ounce/794g) can tomato sauce

1 large egg (aka the single thing I've never been able to offer Jer sexually that his previous partner did)

15 ounces (425g) whole-milk ricotta cheese

1 pound (450g) gluten-free oven-ready lasagna noodles (I recommend chickpea noodles, mostly because our stiffest competition online is always from chick pee videos, and if you can't beat 'em, join 'em.)

1 teaspoon dried Italian seasoning

A level of despair that cannot be fixed

Mozzarella and Parmesan cheese, grated (Go fucking nuts. It's been a long day.)

Method

1. In a medium saucepan set over medium-low heat, add the olive oil and fry up your onions and garlic until they begin to soften, about 2 minutes. Add the meat or meat substitute to the pan and increase the heat to medium. Allow the meat to cook fully, then add ½ teaspoon salt and ½ teaspoon pepper. (Or, as they're known in the

middle of the country, "the spice rack".) Once it's fried and drained, say to it, "Bitch, now you know how I feel!"

2. Add the tomato sauce and ½ cup of water to the pan and stir. It feels wrong to add water, but us neurodivergents love when we're doing something that feels wrong—plus it helps cook the noodles so just fucking trust me. Reduce the heat to low and allow the sauce to simmer for 10 to 15 minutes.

3. Crack the egg into a medium-size mixing bowl and combine it with the ricotta cheese, lightly beating the egg. Don't let the sound this process makes turn you off of the project.

4. Now, it's time to build! BUILD THE CHEESE-SUNDAE OF DESPAIR! Oh shit, did you already preheat the oven to 375°F (190°C)? START THE OVEN NOW! Fuck, that should have been the first step, whoops. My bad, but hey, while you wait for it to warm up you can start washing the other dishes or just go watch three episodes of *The Office* and forget you were hungry/sad in the first place.

5. Welcome back! Michael Scott, so funny right? I'd fuck Jim Halpert so hard. Oh, were some of you watching the British *Office*? Okay, hear me out: not for their personalities but ... Finchy and Neil? Classic secretary fantasy, I'm taking dictation? Anyways, let's build our magma cheese despair layer by layer. Start by spreading about ⅓ to ½ of the meat sauce along the bottom of a 9 x 13-inch (23 x 33cm) pan. [Note to publishers: please change to "trusty Pyrex™ brand dish" if Jer can manage to sell them a shout-out in this section.]

6. Add 4 noodles to cover the sauce, then spread half the ricotta and egg mixture—Fuck! Shit! Sorry! Stop! You should add the Italian seasoning and the remaining ½ teaspoon salt and ½ teaspoon pepper to the ricotta. Or even better, add fresh herbs in place of the dried. I really don't care which spices or herbs, as long as they're Italian. Or just shout something Italian at it like, *"Eh yo, Adrian,*

we did it!" Spread half the ricotta cheese/egg/*Rocky* mixture over the noodles, then spread another cup of the meat sauce

7. NOW CHEESE THAT FUCKER! Spread a whole bunch of cheese over everything. Then add some noodles over that, spread the remaining ricotta/egg/*Rocky* over the noodles, top *IT* with the remaining meat sauce, and then CHEESE THAT FUCKER AGAIN! HARDER!!!

8. I'm sorry, I have to find Jer. Go watch some more *The Office* for a bit.

9. Okay, I'm back. Isn't it sad about Pam and/or Dawn? She should follow her dreams! And you should, too—your cheese dreams! Cover the whole thing with tinfoil and bake for 30 minutes. Now, remove the foil (God, there are so many Americans I want to say this to, and it has nothing to do with lasagna) and bake for 10 more minutes.

10. Then, turn the broiler on—I like to broil the top of the lasagna for about 3 minutes to make it look pretty. Like a savory crème brûlée—only instead of diabetes, it gives you heart disease. Transfer the lasagna to the stove top.

11. Now here's the hardest step of all. And it's also the step that finally convinced my editor to let me include it in a book that was supposed to help people with ADHD: LET IT REST, BITCH! You can't touch it. You can't eat it yet. You have to let it rest for 5 to 10 minutes. Not easy, right? Well what I like to do is just stare at it until I forget my problems. But by then, it's usually cold! So set a timer for 5 minutes and then dive in and eat away while trying to forget that one of your best friends' bodies is being ravaged by a terrible disease. Oh fuck, and here I am again, right back to where we started. Welp, off to get more chickpissin' noodles.

11.5
WHERE WAS I?

A funny thing about grief and about fear—they don't do anything to affect the price of groceries. At this point, I still didn't have a job. The only reed I was clinging to at this point, workwise, was the development deal with CTV. Still desperately worried about Ashley, still fresh off the loss of Sally Field (I'm sorry), I headed to Los Angeles for work on writing the sitcom. This was the show I've dreamt my whole life about making. This was the chance for Jer and me to give Grace the life she deserves. And this was the moment that it came.

As everyone who's ever been there—from wide-eyed naïve writers to midwestern farmers' daughters to the bearded gay sons of ex-Toronto bomb squad guys—will tell you, Hollywood is a seductress. It will draw you in. It's a city of make believe that makes reality fall away, baby. For just a little while, it'll charm all your worries away. That is, until you're sitting across a table from Bruce McCulloch, your potential future showrunner, eternal Kid in the Hall, who asks you, after spending all of just one hour with you *"So, how long have you had ADHD?"*

How long have I had what?

When I finally went home a few days later, it was with Bruce's voice in my head. What did he mean by that? What could have given him the idea that I had ADHD?

I called my parents and asked them, *"Did you ever think I had ADHD when I was a kid?"*

"*No,*" said my dad. "*We just thought you were an asshole—a busy asshole.*" Dad, I love you, and as we've already established, you handled the coming-out talk beautifully; but I am not and never will be ready to talk to you about how busy my asshole is.

Next, I did what everyone else does when they have a medical question—I turned to Google, and folks, it turned out I had eleven minutes to live.

I thought, fuck it, might as well do some more digging with my last eleven minutes ... and there it was. ICEBERG straight ahead! I had found the graphic that would change my life. The graphic that would scream from the heavens, "Hey, homo! Try to focus long enough to actually digest what this is saying!"

WHAT PEOPLE THINK ADHD IS

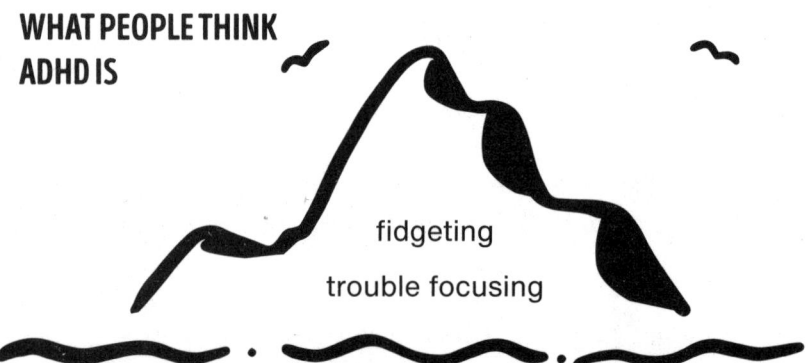

fidgeting

trouble focusing

uncontrollable fidgeting · poor sense of time

inability to focus, even with zero distractions

anxiety · sensory processing disorder

difficulty maintaining relationships

sleeping problems · depression

choice paralysis · poor impulse control

forgetting basic self-care (eat, sleep, etc.)

auditory processing disorder

losing items constantly

inability to stick to a task

forgetting thoughts after having them

difficulty switching tasks

executive dysfunction

hyperfixations

WHAT ADHD ACTUALLY IS

Here's what I knew about ADHD before I found this graphic: there was a kid in my elementary school classroom who would, literally, get up and run laps around the desks while screaming about his love of He-Man. And in fairness, for a while I actually did relate to what this kid was going through, 'cuz He-Man was kind of a babe. But alas, I hadn't realized how much me and this little in-class jogger had in common. I wasn't fast, I wasn't a kid running around—so the whole hyperactive thing just never clicked for me. That is, until the day I googled. And there it was. The iceberg.

By the way, if this seems dramatic, even cinematic, that's because it is! And I don't think this opportunity should be squandered! So that's why I'd like to take this opportunity to address my fellow Canadian, Mr. James Cameron, and say: look, you've already shown that the world will wait a long time for a sequel. Now I think they're ready for another movie with a villainous iceberg! And by the way, that captain was obviously distracted by something!

Anyway, there it was—my Aha! moment. Ugh, I need a new term for this since Oprah and I aren't friends anymore. Okay, it was my ... A-HON HON HON (laughs in French) moment!

Difficulties with impulse control? Tell that to the tandem bike I rode into the set wall! Rejection sensitive dysphoria? HA! Tell that to everyone that's ever seen my act and not laughed because they secretly hated me! Chronic unemployment? Was it? Or was I just ready to move on to the next adventure?

I know it's an iceberg, but if you'll allow me to mix cold metaphors for a second, I need for you, my little readers, to understand the avalanche of emotions this drawing gave me. I was flummoxed. I was floored. I was on the phone to my doctor immediately—this was a dopamine hit that I was going to chase all the way to a diagnosis. Which, in the prepandemic times, wasn't actually too hard.

These days that's not the case; I'm told by friends the waitlist can be twenty-four months long to see a specialist. It's a tragedy. And I will never shame folks that go the route of self-diagnosis because for some it's the only viable route.

But these were the before times, and I live in a country with civilized universal health care. I went down the road of talking to my GP and getting referred to two specialists, and they all came back with the same diagnosis: I had eleven minutes to live.

Or if not, maybe sometimes it would feel that way, because I had a fuck ton of ADHD.

We did a joke in our stand-up special *No Refunds*—available worldwide *cough cough*, especially if you borrowed this book from a friend—that I was super easy to diagnose with ADHD because I missed my assessment appointment four times. (That's just a small taste of the kind of thrills, chills, and spills that await you when you stream *No Refunds*!) But that wasn't actually the case— the reality was that I did in fact miss my first appointment, and then I rescheduled it two more times out of fear. I just couldn't get myself into that room. (See, the true story isn't very funny, is it? And that's why it had no place in *No Refunds*, a wall-to-wall comic romp with your best parasocial friends from the internet! Stream the audio album anywhere you steal your music from!)

Before this appointment, the only other time I had been in a medical office for reasons related to mental health was when I picked up my friend from therapy once and she invited me in to meet her therapist. The setup was just two chairs right across from each other. That was it. No cozy blankets or pillows, not even much art on the walls. There was nowhere to lean or contort your legs into pretzel positions. It was all just so sterile and raw.

As I was gearing up for my ADHD assessment, I just kept picturing that—and no matter how hard I tried I couldn't see myself opening up in a space like that.

Eventually, what finally broke my deadlock was that they said I'd be charged if I didn't go. Well, when it comes to avoiding charges, I'm like Willie Nelson's accountants (by which I only mean to imply that I am always looking for the best deal for my client, in this case, me) so I finally went to the first of my appointments.

I walked in and immediately my worst fears were out the window. There was a couch with a blanket that had this tight quilt-like pattern, and I was instantly happy that I could be comfortable. I sprawled out on the couch and the doctor and I began just by chatting—MY SPECIALTY!

About me! My other specialty!

And boy oh boy was I ever good at chatting, especially when she asked me about my work history. Like, girl, you might need this couch 'cuz here's the story of thirty-seven jobs in thirty-six years.

I guess with the right environment, I really was able to just relax a bit and lean into why I was there, even though we both knew within the first ten minutes why I was there. It wasn't nearly as scary as I had built it up to be in my mind. We talked about relationships, work, stress, and all the sundry things that involved my brain. All the while, I could quietly play with the quilted blanket in my fingers, and flop from side to side of the magnificent couch.

It wasn't some climactic moment of discovery or big "does he or doesn't he" reveal. It was just us calmly going through my history.

After my first session we were both aware that ADHD was very much my diagnosis, but I couldn't leave after just one session—I'm very entertaining to talk to and she was clearly having a good time taking my money. So we had a few more sessions where I got to learn about myself, my patterns, and my cycles. Basically, it was like getting this book, for about ten times the price per week. From there, I could start to recognize those behaviors and tendencies in the future to prevent repetition.

Which is why I've never had any challenges or confusions or difficulties since. Shit, I wonder what we're gonna do for the rest of the book?

WHAT DOES THIS MEAN FOR YOU?

Knowing is growing! Sorry, I'll try not to have any more rhyming advice. But chances are, the fears and anxieties preventing you from finding out what is or isn't going on with you might actually be way worse than what you're going to find out! (Also just so we're absolutely clear here, I consider myself to be both a knower and a grower; ask Jer.)

CHOOSE YOUR OWN DISTRACTION

- → If you want to read about Europe's hottest ADHD-friendly destinations, turn to page 190.
- → If you want to read about America's hottest ADHD-friendly destinations, turn to page 225.
- → If you want to learn how to mostly ignore a life-changing discovery and find the bottom under rock bottom, keep reading ...

12.
ADHD & ROCK BOTTOM

DARCY GOES TO CHURCH. GOD IS WATCHING SOMETHING ELSE.

With the benefit of hindsight and my new diagnosis, at this point the puzzle pieces should probably have started to slide into place. There should probably have been a new clarity about old patterns and recurring challenges. New vistas and horizons, whatever vistas are. Instead, I just took some pills and mostly filed it away.

Why did I do that? I'm not sure I have the self-awareness even now to say entirely why—I may be a doll, but I ain't the Dalai Lama, and at any given moment, even my own motivations and stumbling blocks aren't always fully transparent to me. What I really remember from that time was a distinct impression that ... life just kinda sucked right then.

I was going through a sort of backward grieving process after receiving my diagnosis; something that a lot of people experience after receiving an adult assessment of ADHD. On the one hand, there's a wonderful feeling that certain big swathes of life suddenly make sense, whereas before they just didn't add up. With that exhilaration comes an excitement about all the new possibilities that the future may hold now that you know what's going on.

But pretty quickly, that grooving about the future slips ass backward into a memorial service for the past. Before I knew what hit me, I was looking back on all the failed school assignments, the jobs I'd left, the friendships I ruined, all with a kind of deep, heavy fear about how sure, maybe I've survived this long—but I was starting to think that I probably hadn't been thriving.

Then into this deep, dark existential well came a call from my pal Zoe at Just for Laughs. The well part is a metaphor; I was just in Ladner. But she really did call—specifically, to ask me if I thought I was ready to film my own stand-up comedy special to stream across the country.

Um, EXCUSE ME, WHAT?!?!? I think I just streamed across the country myself, Zoe.

Diagnosis, shmiagshmosis! Thriving, shmiving! Self-awareness, shmelf-ashmareness! All that broody, dark berets and cigarettes, what-does-it-all-mean shit went straight out the window and Darcy Michael ran straight to the airport. And let me remind you, for me to do anything straight is quite exceptional.

Honestly, where did I even get off, questioning whether or not I was thriving? I mean, here I was, being selected as the very first comedian in Canada to get my own full-length, streaming network stand-up special in Canada for Crave TV ... and they wanted to film it in a church! HON HON HON, mais oui, mon ami! I'm in! Finally, this was my moment!

I filmed *Darcy Michael Goes to Church* in the Berkeley Church building in Toronto. The entire incredible, imposing, decommissioned Victorian-era church was full of all my friends and family. Jer and Grace even joined me on stage for my bow at the end of the show. They were so nervous, it was adorable. There was absolutely no sign yet in Jer of the irrepressible little footlights whore that he would one day become.

This wasn't anything like my *Comedy Now!* taping experience. There was no negotiating to be allowed to wear a hat; there was no stretching my material to see if I could get it to cover a full twenty-two minutes. This wasn't standing on a cheap afterthought stage set (that looked like what some 1980s Sicilian businessman might have thought the 2010s would look like, all backlit smooth surfaces in various pastels) that also doubled as the set of the network's equally inexpensive Canadian improv show. This time, the set could not have been more beautiful—funky, otherworldly, and imposing in the best, most incongruous way. The set looked great; and I looked fantastic. I was no longer at my emaciated skinniest—I just looked healthy and happy, but not so much that the audience wouldn't laugh this time.

And I was at the height of my powers as a stand-up. I told real stories, from real places—I shared my coming-out story onstage, I talked about being a gay father, and I did it all in the city where I had lived some of the first truly open and free months of my life as a young gay man. It was true. It was funny. It was me.

And ... it just didn't fucking matter.

People with ADHD are often overcome by a strong, terrifying feeling that life is simply slipping through their fingers. But this time it didn't seem like a feeling. This time I really did appear to be incapable of holding onto anything that really mattered.

As the editing work neared completion on the special, the network began to tap me on the shoulder for my upcoming publicity. But by this time, I was back home, and Ashley's condition had badly deteriorated. I was trying to be at her bedside as much as was allowed. Whenever I wasn't at her side, I was pretending to be happy and funny on tour dates and doing promotion for the special. CTV, to their credit, gave it a full court press run; I spent a day in Toronto doing basically all the press in Canada promoting the special. But the entire time I was also a world away, in my mind, worrying about

Ashley. Worrying about the friend who had been there in the audience at every single show I'd ever done in Vancouver, in my home city, from the most glamorous stadium gigs opening for the likes of Russell Peters right down to the half-empty back rooms of eastside Cuban restaurants.

Darcy Michael Goes to Church was released, and Russian cosmonauts at the international space station could hear the silence.

No one watched.

Which is not to say that no one paid any attention. CTV certainly did. And I guess because no one watched my special, the network was starting to have second thoughts about whether I should have a sitcom based on my life. And yet, I'm almost certain—in fact, I'm quite sure—that I could have handled any of this. If.

If Ashley hadn't died.

But she did.

She died.

And I was obliterated. I was inconsolable.

On the day of her celebration of life, a soft rain fell out of the gray Vancouver sky, the kind of weather that becomes a sort of wallpaper sadness for whole stretches of the year. I took the microphone from her husband, my friend and my frequent collaborator Tom Belding, and spoke to a standing-room-only gathering of Ashley's friends, family, and loved ones in the Stanley Park Tea Room. I tried to say at least a few funny things through my tears, because it's what my beautiful friend would have wanted.

The next night, over dinner with representatives from CTV, I was informed that the sitcom development deal was over. The dream was finished before it started.

And I barely felt a thing.

Here's what I've learned about the real rock bottom: If you're even thinking about how to get back up again, you're not there.

Once you get to the real rock bottom … you'd just as soon stay down.

I don't think I'm going to offer a choice of distraction this time or neatly bundle up the take-away gems, okay? We're all just going to talk about plants.

13.
ADHD & THE ROAD NOT TAKEN

PLANTS LIVE IN ONE PLACE, AND A STAR FEEDS THEM

We're going to take a break here, okay? I know that it's quite possible that right now you're on a roll, having a ton of momentum getting this book finished, and if that's the case, I'm very happy for you; I really couldn't be more pleased. But you know what? Not to put too fine a point on it, but you're not the only one trying to get through this frigging thing, okay? Maybe finishing this book is starting to kick the shit out of me a little bit, alright? Maybe when they came and told me I was going to be a published author, I was so excited about getting my overstuffed wingback chair and sequined playsuit with leather elbow patches that I didn't stop to consider how it might actually feel to make the leap from producing two-to-five-minute internet videos about the adorable foibles of my marriage to sitting down and writing thousands of words of black and white prose about some of the worst memories of my life.

So ... we're going to talk about a few different plants that I think are great starter plants for people looking to bring more greenery into their lives and homes.

Let's start with a pothos plant, the beautiful, brilliant greenie with the leaves in a shape halfway between a heart and a spade—in my opinion, the very easiest plant to grow. Why? They don't care about things like direct sunlight; they love to be forgotten about for weeks on end and then smothered and drowned with water and then forgotten about all over again. These things are to the world of houseplants what Canadian stand-up comedians are to the world of show business. I have a pothos; her name is Blanche, and I have had her for twenty-four years. She's a clipping of my mother's pothos plant. I named her Blanche because she's a little vixen who has birthed hundreds of pothos babies that I give to people whenever they come over. She has spread her seed across Canada and back again. Blanche is a slut, and I love her for it.

Another great plant is a spider plant. They give off little spider babies at a rate that sometimes makes even Blanche blush. And, like a pothos, they don't require much attention while still giving beautiful green and white foliage that helps to clean the air in your room. Not that we're getting back into this, but if you ever were to find yourself in a time and place when both the professional and the personal wings of your life collapsed simultaneously, having a few air-scrubbing spider plants sucking some of the carbon dioxide, failure, and despair out of the air can be a godsend.

Next up is the snake plant. This one is terrific, as long as you forget it exists; the moment the snake plant thinks you're thinking about her, she's dead. So go slowly with her, spit on her roots once a month, and keep her pot tight. She's like me, trying to fit into size 32 jeans when she should be in size 36. Okay, 38. Okay, a muumuu.

Now, I know what you're thinking: "Spider-plant, snake-plant ... Darcy, why do all of these plants have to be named after the most terrifying creatures on the planet?" Well, first of all, with that attitude I'm never going to tell you about covid-bat plants. But secondly, they're just names! And I'm trying to set you up with all of the best plants for people with ADHD—the plants that evolved with natural buffer zones and grace periods; the sturdy little fuckers that Mother Nature sent out into the world in order to cut the easily distracted some slack.

Plants have this magical hold over me; they serve to ground me and at times they even humble me. (I know, that's hard to believe but trust me, I'm so good at being humble and even better at growing plants!) There's a movie from 2000 called *28 Days* starring Sandra Bullock in which her character goes through the process of sobriety. At one point, her sober coach tells her that once she can keep a plant alive for six months, she can move on to dating. I don't know why, but that always stuck with me. All the care on earth hadn't been able to keep Ashley alive, but with plants I could start somewhere smaller. A few extra plants around the house would keep me motivated to keep moving forward ... or at least keep me running away from Jer whenever he saw new plants appear.

Plants are quiet, but they need love, and they need attention. (I should know the type, I married somebody a little like that.) But most will thrive with light and care. We'll get back to the book soon, okay? But this is about ADHD too, I swear. Remember when I said Jer brought peace and stillness into my life for the first time? Well ... I could have worked in a garden center, a little plant store. I don't mean hypothetically, or that I know enough about plants to do it—I mean that at this point in my life, when everything felt finished, that idea seemed to me to make the most sense. To open up a little flower shop in Ladner. To find pleasure in the day to day.

Both plants and performers feed on being in the light. But whereas this life I had been chasing was always taking me away, always moving me, always immersing me in a stream of overstimulation and too much distance from the people most important to me, plants let their roots go further and further every day into the soil of the only place they need to be. Plants are alive—but they're still. They're still—but they're thriving.

Sorry, this part isn't very funny. But I guess that's kind of the point. At first, the budding realization was so delicate, it took some time even to be able to admit to myself. But in time, I was able to share it with Jer, and that was what made it all real.

I had been given my chance. My chances. I had come so close to living my dream that it was almost more painful than if I'd just failed completely. I'd been through RSD before, but this felt different. The world had seen what I had to offer, and time after time, they'd politely turned me down. (I mean, it was still Canada.)

Leaving my husband and my daughter behind for this dream that just kept on rejecting me no longer made any sense—especially when the real dream was them.

I was ready to be around plants. I was ready to be a plant.

I told Jer that I was ready to move on from this part of my life; that I was ready to no longer be a comedian.

But to properly mark the closing of one chapter and the opening of another, a decision like this called for a burst of ADHD money-management carnage the likes of which we'd never seen.

WHAT DOES THIS MEAN FOR YOU?

You're going to have to sort that one out on your own, I think. But don't do it without reading what comes next, okay?

CHOOSE YOUR OWN DISTRACTION

- → To read more of my adventures with a very particularly beloved plant, turn to page 60.

- → If you want to read the story of how my comedy career began, turn to page 105.

- → If you want to read about the biggest credit-fueled stimulus package to hit Europe since the Marshall Plan, keep reading ...

14.
ADHD & TRAVEL
THE WHIRLED TOUR

Okay creeps, it's listicle time! And what better way to buoy flagging ADHD attention than with travel tips?

Tip #1

When planning a trip to a foreign destination—or better yet, a sparkling constellation of destinations!—it's best to do zero research at all (and leave your passport at home, too, while you're at it).

SIDE BAER

OR have a spouse or travel companion who does all the legwork for you so you can just float on by, experiencing the vacation magic.

Sure. That works, too.

So let me set the scene. Here we were: I was officially, but quietly, retired from comedy. I had no source of income for the foreseeable future, no specific plans for next steps, and my only vague long-term idea (to own my own plant store) was extremely capital intensive. So we did what any normal, responsible folks would do under the circumstances. We planned a trip to Europe!

It all made a sick kind of sense, really. Since my ADHD was now cured by ... uh ... having been diagnosed; my depression from finally, definitively losing out on my lifelong dream had been hammered into irrelevance by the pain of losing a best friend; the pain of losing a best friend had been sublimated by a growing (get it?) addiction to plants that spelled ruin for me financially; and my financial woes had been mooted by the fact of my not having any income whatsoever in the first place ... let's rack up a bunch of debt to go to Europe! Aufregend!

Okay, here's the thing: the truth is that after Ashley passed, her beautiful and beloved husband Tom finally went on a trip around Europe that they had always wanted to do together but never could. And his going made me realize that Jer and I had spent eighteen years daydreaming about having the time or the money to go to Europe together. Now we had time but no money. One out of two ain't bad, right? I didn't care. It was happening—we were going to go to Europe together while we could, and by God, we were gonna have fun, damn it!

SIDE BAER

The Eurozone has never been associated with any debt crises, right?

Yes, it was reckless. Listen, here are some good reasons to buy this book:

You want to learn more about what it's like to live with ADHD and/or a man who plays video games and with whom you can have sex.

You're trying to encourage TikTok to take a more literary turn.

You want to financially support a Canadian bear, but you think that the polar has been morally compromised by its ties to the Coca-Cola corporation.

There are centipedes in your basement suite and you need something light enough to swat with but substantial enough to make an impact.

The algorithm says so.

But a very, very bad reason for buying this book would be any kind of search for financial advice. I am not by any means suggesting that you go on an entirely credit-funded multicountry international vacation; that is a decision between you and your interest rate. But there we were, with cards in our hands, aloft above our heads, ready to set off for a big adventure from London to Amsterdam to Barcelona—and yes, goddammit, I pronounced it "Barthelona" like a cocky little shit as I typed this out, and I'd do it again in a second.

SIDE BAER

[Eyeroll audible in Spanish]

You mean like an ¡Aye! ¡Roll!?

[Eyes quit, fall out of sockets]

Now when you're in a same-sex relationship, you often get really cringey inquiries from people about which roles one or the other person plays vis à vis the other. I know it's typical to tell children that "there are no stupid questions," but may I submit that the person who came up with that aphorism had never been asked, "So, which one of you is the girl?" Like all relationships, gay ones are dynamic and fluid, with each member resisting easy, reductive, one-dimensional categories.

Except when we're traveling. When we're traveling, Jer is Daddy.

This may come as a surprise to some of you, but I am actually not the best traveler; I get anxious, I get really weary on long plane rides, and I get hangry as all hell. Jer, however, is what we all like to refer to as an Airport Dad—he has us at our gate seven days in advance with a backpack full of gluten-free snacks and magnetic travel-size board games. He oversees the travel experience as though he has a toddler with him. Because he has a toddler with him. A giant, bearded toddler.

Starting the trip with only twenty-four hours in London, we did the thing I never thought we would ever do: a hop-on hop-off bus tour. I always figured them to be so cheesy and touristy, but then I remembered that Jer and I were cheesy tourists, and boy did it ever change my idea of seeing a city. It was the perfect London day (and by that I mean it was pouring rain and everyone was grumpy). I loved every minute of it—the city was so fun and packed to the rafters with history. And who knew, but the constant hopping on and hopping off was feeding my dopamine like a perfect ADHD field trip. Highly recommended for the neurofabulous!

I remember us taking a picture under London Bridge (happily, the song was totally inaccurate), Thames-wide smiles on our faces just from the fact that we had finally made it to London. It was a magical start to the trip, and then the icing on the London cake—the chutney on the kebab, the second deck on the bus—was when we did the typical gay thing and went to the West End, walked up to a ticket booth, and asked, "What show would you go to if you could tonight?" The girl read our gay faces and immediately suggested *There's Something About Jamie*—a musical about a gay kid with dreams of being a drag queen. To me, the very premise of this show raised a philosophical question: could something be so gay that it goes all the way around and becomes straight again? Answer: no. Like, really no. I fucking loved London already. Plus, as if that wasn't enough, we found gluten-free chicken nuggets. I really fucking loved London.

Next, we hopped on a train to go to AMSTERDAM! And this is the part of the book where I regale you with all our fun stories of Amsterdam, but truthfully I can't remember it at all. It's a real catch-22: in a book by a stoner with ADHD, you naturally want all the details about his trip to Amsterdam—but if he's a genuine ADHD stoner, Amsterdam is the one city he's never coming back with memories of.

It's all a dreamy blur, besides the part where we got off the train and found a store that sold magic truffles. Now, did the man say to us, *"Don't eat food while you have truffles in your system?"* Yes, he did. And did we listen to him? To a degree.

SIDE BAER

Some people go to Amsterdam's Red Light District. Clearly, we got stuck in the Red Flag District.

Oh, you loved it.

Jer and I embarked on a five-day adventure of walking the city while tripping our balls off. But as one does in Europe, we wanted to taste the local cuisine. So as we walked our way around town, I saw a sign that was clearly not in English and yet, in all my truffled glory, I swore I could read and comprehend the Dutch for gluten-free. In we walked to this magical local specialty restaurant, full of joy. I approached the counter and asked in clear, precise, not-at-all-high truffle language, *"Do you have gluten-free cheeseburgers?"*

"Yes."

A single tear drop rolled down my cheek.

"Thank you," I said. *"I'll have eight, please."*

And we sat down in this foreign land to try the magical gluten-free cheeseburger cuisine being offered by these quaint European artisans.

SIDE BAER
It was a fucking McDonalds, Darcy.

Shhhh, details don't matter. Not in Trufflelopolis. What matters is that I had not had a cheeseburger from this wonderful place in over ten years. And I was going to savor every bite—shit, where'd they go? Fuck, I ate them all? Well, it's okay, we'll be back tomorrow to try more fine Dutch cuisine.

We would not be back.

You see, dear reader, as I so coyly foreshadowed all of three and a half paragraphs ago, I was not supposed to eat food while on magic truffles and yet, there I was—full of cheeseburgers. You can see the conundrum. Gluten-free or not, something was happening. Truffles or not, something not altogether magic. And it wasn't just for me; Jer, too, had a look on his face that said we can't be in public for this next part.

SIDE BAER

Did I ever officially agree to be in this book?

For better or for worse, bitch!

So Jer being Jer, and since in Amsterdam public toilets cost money, and our hotel was only ten minutes away, he insisted that we would do the responsible thing (gotta start somewhere, right?) and walk back to our place. Surely we could make it, right? It's way better to have the privacy of one's own hotel room, not to mention all those sweet euros we'd be saving on the public toilet.

Anyway, I shat myself thirty seconds into the walk.

SIDE BAER

Love that European sophistication.

Now look, there was obviously some impulse-control stuff going on here and clearly some pretty heavy dopamine-digging, so you may be inclined to lay the blame for my dirty drawers at the feet of ADHD. But I will remind you that Jer almost shat himself, too.

On magic truffles, no one is neurotypical!

TIP #2

If you want an excuse to buy new pants, eat magic truffles and head to McDonalds!

We really loved Amsterdam. Drugs aside, that city and its country's history for gay rights is unmatched. It goes as far back as decriminalizing homosexuality in 1811 (or was that canal sex?) and having its first openly gay bar in 1927. (Now that's how you make the twenties roar.) I truly felt so safe and welcomed, it was a magical experience. Walking down the beautiful streets along the canals, holding Jer's hand (don't worry, after shitgate, I washed my hands), I felt the spark coming back a bit. We were completely in the moment with each other. Our phones didn't have data, so it was just the two of us, present, together. Sometimes shitting ourselves.

Five days later Jeremy dragged me kicking and screaming to our next adventure. I never wanted to leave, but here we were on our way to Barthelona. (It's not cultural appropriation if a gay guy lisps.)

We landed in the city and soon found ourselves standing on La Rambla, a tree-lined pedestrian street stretching for three-quarters of a mile (1.2 kilometers) between the Plaça de Catalunya and the Christopher Columbus Monument at Port Vell. (In 2019, the Spaniards had not yet gotten the memo about Columbus monuments.)

It was here, in this moment of us being lost and unable to find our hotel, surrounded by the smells of every restaurant and the sounds of every tourist, musician, garbage truck, and every other noise known to man, that I started to clue in to the fact that perhaps I was suffering a sensory overload? Is this wave of panic that was causing me to freeze up completely and utterly shut down something new? No, it wasn't—when I considered it for a second, I realized it was actually something that had been happening my entire life. But now that I had that stupid fucking ADHD iceberg graphic in my head, I could refer back to it and think: Wowza! Darcy don't likey this.

And so, I thought I was going to hate Barcelona. And then ... we found our hotel. A hotel that shall remain nameless, but let me just say that this was the one and only hotel on our entire trip that I, rather than Jer, had booked for us. I had been so proud when I found this quaint little five-story walk-up in the Barcelona gayborhood that offered a gay stay like no other. And boy oh boy, were they right!

You see, I had booked us at a gay swingers' hotel. That's right. The room came with three signs for hanging on the doorknob that roughly translated to:

1. "Do Not Disturb"
2. "Please clean my room"
3. "Welcome to pound town, come fuck my face"

Like I said, a rough translation ... but as we walked to our room, we did notice another room's door slightly ajar, and on it was hung sign #3 and inside it was ... hung.

We googled the Spanish for "not our vibe"—but even "no es nuestra vibra" sounds a little too much like a sex toy for our liking.

Alas, we prepaid—so we were staying here for two nights and moving on.

I know I'm complaining about Barcelona, but a mature person would maybe point out that—

SIDE BAER

Don't worry, I'm here for this moment. You see, Darcy's sensory overload panic attack was due to poor planning on our transportation—not the fault of Barcelona.

Ahem. BARTHELONA.

Insert eye roll here. And then, again, our hotel, um ... mix up was not the fault of Barcelona.

BARTHELONA!

You really meant it when you said you retired from comedy, huh?

Fine. We actually loved walking all over the city and exploring for days. The one thing we couldn't get over was how great they were at every restaurant for food allergies. Europe does it right.

When it comes to food, Jer and I are little old ladies. We eat dinner early; I think it started from years of touring—I would eat a little dinner around 4 or 5 p.m., then head out to my show. And now, as a retiree, I wanted my dinner at 4 p.m. But Spanish siesta culture was all, "No, fatty! You eat when we are done napping!"

So there Jer and I were, every night at 8 p.m. sharp waiting for something, ANYTHING, to open for us to eat.

It was on one of these nights that for the first time in two weeks, we started talking to another couple at the bar. After fourteen LOVING days together, we were both very much ready to talk to other people. Anyhow, fast forward to the drunkest we've ever been in our lives, we skipped dinner and bar-hopped with Person 1 and Person 2—we never got their names and can't tell you a thing about them other than the fact that they liked Jäger bombs as much as we (thought) we did.

The next morning we were supposed to take a forty-minute train ride to Sitges. We did not make the train. Jeremy insists to this day that he is still hungover from that night.

SIDE BAER

Do you have to type so loudly?

So instead, we took a leisurely-if-sometimes-rough taxi ride to Sitges to check into our beachfront hotel for a week. A friend from our tennis club had suggested this little town as a great place to kick back and enjoy some coastal living.[1] We had neglected to register the significance of the fact that this friend of ours from our tennis club was gay. We did not realize this kindly older gentleman, who wintered here every year, was, in fact, a homosexual.

---

1   I know this makes it sound like we had money, but the tennis club was on the credit cards, too.

Potentially, as it turned out, the world champion of homosexuality. It was as we walked down this one particularly cute little alley toward our hotel, that we noticed that every building was flying rainbow flags, and, in our fragile state of extreme hangover, we also found ourselves both suddenly overwhelmed by the smell of bleach. And that's when we strolled past a nightclub called Bukkake.

Now if you don't know what the term "bukkake" is, this isn't the moment to google it. Trust me, don't. Just take my word for it: the bleach made sense. We had come to a gay cruising town and, judging by the industrial cleaners, it was prime tourist season!

We actually loved having quiet days strolling the beach, eating at 8 p.m. sharp, and going to bed before the bars got too busy or Mr. Clean had to get to scrubbing. We went to the nude beach and stripped off our clothes and ran into the ocean to swim and have silly little romantic kisses and laugh uncontrollably at how much fun this entire trip had been.

I was healing. We were healing. I felt myself again, and I felt myself more in love with Jeremy than ever before. Here we were, after years of fighting against the current, finding ourselves together, just the two of us. Grace was off to college, Jer had a good job, and I had some shit to figure out, but I was ready to put the work in. This trip was worth every penny Jer spent.

The trip put into perspective the things that had hurt which were actually small and not worth worrying about; and the hurt that was real, from losing Ashley, felt more bearable because we had each other. Whatever came next, we could face it.

In fact, our 2019 trip was so soul renewing, we knew how we'd be telling all our friends to spend 2020: travel, travel, travel!

WHAT DOES THIS MEAN FOR YOU?

Here are Darcy's real life, no-foolin' ADHD travel tips, good for hauling ass over the long haul:

- Use a packing checklist. And I mean every single time. Future You will thank Past You for treating your brain like a rental car.
- Set multiple alarms. For wake-up, check-out, "leave now or miss your flight," and "stop getting distracted by airport snacks."
- Packing cubes = fewer meltdowns. Organize by category: clothes, chargers, and random anxiety meds you forgot you were prescribed.
- Duplicate your essentials. Toothbrush, charger, meds—keep a travel set always ready to go in your bag. Also handy if you or a loved one are about to go into labor!
- Screenshots > memory. Boarding passes, hotel info, gate numbers—screenshot it all like your brain is about to crash (because it is).
- Set a reminder to take your meds. Then set another to remind you what that first reminder was for.
- Bring sensory tools. Noise-canceling headphones, fidget toys, gum. Or a hoodie you can disappear into like a feral raccoon.
- Use the Notes app as your external brain. Grocery list? Terminal number? Which one's your hotel room? Dump it all in there.
- Schedule wiggle time. You will need a dance break in a rest stop bathroom at some point. Plan accordingly.

- Put an AirTag in your suitcase. And in your carry-on. And maybe in your spouse. Trust no one.

- Talk to yourself in public like you're your own personal assistant. "Alright, babe, keys? Wallet? Dignity? Let's do this."

- Pack snacks or you'll commit crimes. No one wants to see what happens when you're hangry, overstimulated, and stranded in a Hudson News.

- Wear a fanny pack like a tactical ADHD utility belt. Fill it with gum, lip balm, cash, and three mystery objects you'll forget are in there until 2032.

- Announce your current task out loud like you're filming a vlog. "We are now walking to the boarding gate and NOT stopping at Cinnabon. Not. Stopping."

- Bring a "chaos bag." It's just where you throw all the loose crap you don't want to deal with. This is sacred. Do not question The Chaos Bag.

- Every thirty minutes, ask yourself: What was I doing again? Not to actually find out—just to stay humble.

- Give your suitcase a name so you'll feel bad if you lose it. "Come on, Linda. Don't get left at baggage claim again."

- Reward yourself with stickers or candy like you're five. Because let's be real—you still are, emotionally.

CHOOSE YOUR OWN DISTRACTION

→ If you want to know what it's like when we travel for work instead of pleasure, turn to page 218.

→ If you want to read about one of my very first road trips, turn to page 68.

→ If you want to hear about what happens when the shutdown of the whole world meets the power of hyperfixation, keep reading ...

EUROPE'S TOP 10 ADHD TOURIST DESTINATIONS

The Eiffel Platform—Paris, France

Too many of Paris's millions of visitors overlook Gustave Eiffel's other great nineteenth-century metalwork, an 8-foot platform in his signature iron. The 11 steps here are just as good as any of the 674 you're allowed to climb at the tower, making the platform an ideal spot for tourists who "fucking get it already with the stairs."

Mistress Ageeth's RSD-Kink Dungeon—Amsterdam Red Light District, Holland

Infamously severe dominatrix Mistress Ageeth reduces her rejection sensitive clientele to quivering piles of jelly with thrilling punishments like smiling at jokes instead of laughing and sending texts with periods instead of exclamation points. Bottoms up!

Musée d'Objets Transitoire—Brussels, Belgium

This Belgian museum of object permanence is totally unforgettable (unless you leave it).

Il Museo Della Cronometria Antifascista—Turin, Italy

Just because the brutal dictatorship of Benito Mussolini built its identity around "making the trains run on time" doesn't necessarily mean that people who stick to a schedule are fascists. It does, however, mean that people who are late are heroes of anti-fascism, as the Museum of Anti-Fascist Timekeeping makes clear in their incredible exhibits. Hours vary.

Pavillion of Hermes—Corinth, Greece

I'm going to be honest, I was looking for a fancy watch. But as it happens, Hermes was the ancient Greek messenger God, associated with speed, and his sweet little booties with the wings on the ankle are such an obvious ADHD fantasy I could just die.

Duncan's Impatience—Teith River, Scotland

Visit the location where brave warriors for the sovereignty of the Scottish king, led by Lord Duncan, found a perfect series of caves in which to lie entirely hidden in wait for enemy English troops before ultimately losing patience and getting caught climbing down for a snack.

Zeitblindheitserfahrung—Berlin, Germany

Zeitblindheitserfahrung is the single German word meaning "the time-blindness experience." Only the Germans can manage to be efficient in their ADHD.

The Twitch & Fiddle—Somerset, England

Britain's oldest fidget-based pub (est. 1132)

The Wandering of the Bulls—Pamplona, Spain

Less fuss, less muss—yes, más! The running of the bulls gets all the headlines, but it also gets all the casualties. The wandering of the bulls is much slower paced, less directed, and tends just to sort of dissipate organically without a big to-do. Still lots of cute red kerchiefs.

Hand Job Paddy Power-Betting Parlor—Sligo, Ireland

I jerked a guy off in the bathroom after he won ninety euros betting off-track horseraces. I guess it's sort of ADHD-adjacent because he did seem distracted.

15.
ADHD & HOUSEHOLD PETS

3:10 TO YUMA DOG

Fresh off the high of our amazing overseas adventure and still smelling like Europe (the unbleached parts), feeling a spark in my soul that I thought had died a few months earlier, Jer and I returned home ready to tackle the next adventure. Given the plant-shelter fantasies that I'd been entertaining before we'd left, the safe bet on our next adventure was that it would involve the middle category of animal, vegetable, or mineral. But no, instead, our loving cat of eighteen years, Felicia Gallant (shout out to anyone that gets this *Another World* reference), was dying and the day after we got home, we had to say goodbye to my little friend. The hits kept coming. The night after Felicia left us was our first night together in our own home with no pets or children in all of our years together. It was so quiet; it was so sad.

Now, I want to clear up a couple of quick things before proceeding. First of all, and I think this should go without saying, but: Felicia was not dying because we'd forgotten to feed her while we were in Europe. I have ADHD, not a full frontal lobotomy. She was being looked after while we were gone—she was eighteen years old, for fuck's sake, she could practically vote; we knew how to keep her alive. But the other thing I want to clear up is that my editor says this is the first time I've brought up Felicia, and since she hasn't come up in any of the other stories I've told about the preceding eighteen years, it makes it sound like I didn't really love her to bits. I am very sorry, but that is just an extremely dog-person thing to say. And I can say that, because I'm a dog person, too. But in this era of extreme polarization, we need more voices of moderation, more people like Jer and me—cat people who are also dog people, dog people who are also cat people—who can see both sides of the issue and speak with loving empathy to both sets of experiences. I'm Darcy Michael, and I approve this message.

Yeah, if I had a dog for eighteen years, and they hadn't come up in the book yet? That would be psychotic. I'm totally with you. But a cat is a horse of a completely different color. (Figuratively; we have an excellent public school system here in Canada and my inability to concentrate during biology wasn't that crippling.) A cat is more like a downstairs neighbor who keeps a dish and a couple of toys at your place and very occasionally comes around for a little snuggle. (I don't know if that analogy will be relatable for straight readers, but hopefully you read the bit about the Spanish hotel so you can piece it together.) The fact that I haven't brought up Felicia before now is merely a tribute to her dignified life of aloof independence.

In ADHD terms: dogs are a set of cognitive-behavioral therapy (CBT) interventions—like a series of alarm reminders and naturally-occurring schedule structures, dogs will insist on walks and games and food and attention at specific points during the day, every day, throughout their lives. Dogs are a treatment animal. Cats, on the other hand, are an ADHD mirror. Half the time you don't know where they are; they pick at their food over the course of hours, grazing instead of having structured meals; they're always at work on some cockamamie project that they can't really explain to you.

Let me put it this way: if shaky object permanence ever affected my relationship with Felicia, it was probably hers.

So Felicia's death hit us hard. I never knew I could be so sad about a pillow that snored, but here I was, sad again! So much fun for a comedy book, right? I promise I won't kill anyone else off before the end of this book. I don't think? Object permanence and grief can be hard, so I might have forgotten one more death, but I really do think this is it. My next book? No guarantees.

But we didn't get long to sit with Felicia's passing, because the next day my mom called me in a panic, explaining between hyperventilations that they had to go to Toronto because my grandmother was sick. ARE YOU FUCKING KIDDING ME.

The complicating factor was that my parents now had a four-month-old golden retriever named Charlee (she's a girl, she's just different), and could we look after her for two weeks while they were away?

CAN WE?

Yes fucking please. Give me something, anything, to distract me from the misery of my empty, lifeless home.

SIDE BAER

Excuse me?

You know what I mean! Empty and lifeless when I'm not around. (Don't worry, I'll put down that you're rolling your eyes for the record.) After the Sally Field experience, Jer was hesitant about dogs. But the following two hilarious and chaotic weeks of having a puppy all but sold the both of us on the idea that the specific joy these furry little goobers bring was a joy we were ready to try for again.

SIDE BAER

Sally gave me some PTSD with dogs for sure, but seeing the spark that Charlee was giving to Darcy was all I needed to know that yes, we're ready for a dog, and yes, it had to be a golden retriever.

This is when Yuma—named after (real-life shithole) Yuma, Arizona—came into our lives.

I wanted to name her Yuma because it's the sunniest place in the world, despite being an actual dump. I also really liked saying Yuma Dog ... the joke might not scan because this is a book, so you're going to have to pull your weight here. Yuma Dog. Get it now? Like ... oh, for fuck's sake, YOU MY DOG.

Yuma was just what I needed and one of the sweetest hyperfixations I've ever had. She calmed me down like Jer and plants have for all these years, but she also gave me a new lease on life. Basically, I'm saying if you're neurodiverse and sad, get a fucking golden retriever. And if you're feeling adventurous, maybe throw some mushrooms in the mix. For you, not the dog! AND NEVER TRUFFLES. (But for God's sake if you do, bring the poop bags.)

With the puppy in the house, I found myself jumping out of bed every day—mostly because Yuma was shitting on the floor, but also because I was just so excited and filled with a sense of purpose. I had this beautiful goofball to keep entertained, and trained, and walked. And walked. And so many fucking walks. Puppies are a lot! Like, almost too much? But she's my sunshine on a leash, so there I was in the dead of November rain, walking her for the fifteenth time that day and just begging her to shit.

Now the great news is, all the things that are good for dogs—things like structure and long walks—are good for people with ADHD. The ... other? ... news is, if you think my ADHD was bad before, meet the golden retriever puppy—ADHD on four legs. But not chill, inattentive ADHD, like the cat. We're talking the kid from my elementary school class running laps around the desks.

SIDE BAER
Sometimes I wonder if Yuma's ADHD is more nurture over nature.

I assume that my Corporate Stooge is referring to all the time our pooch spends online.

Actually no, I was—

A non-minor byproduct of Yuma's entry into our lives was that I wanted to share videos of the pooch with our friends and family. I didn't know how to edit videos, but someone on one of my three thousand walks one day mentioned that they had something called a TikTok channel for their dog and they loved it. I began to explain how I couldn't stomach ticks, and when Yuma got them I had to wait for my husband to get home to pull them out, but he patiently explained that no, TikTok was an app where you could upload multiple videos and share them easily with friends. It was all new to me, but what was retirement for if not adventures like these? So I downloaded the app and started the channel YumaDog.

I innocently started a TikTok channel for Yuma so my friends and family could watch her silly little antics. I loved playing the game of "You steal it, you wear it!" but eventually instead of socks and facecloths, she brought me a frying pan, which oddly served as a great reminder that I had started cooking eggs two hours before … luckily for me, Yuma had cleaned up the eggs before bringing me the pan.

As luck would have it, I found myself enjoying putting together a little daily video post on her TikTok channel. As she started to grow, and her training started to take shape, the one thing I couldn't get this dog to do was leave a rock alone. Yuma loves to rock. And by that I mean, scream at the top of her very high-pitched valley girl bark while pushing a rock, rolling on a rock, tossing a rock—whatever it is, she's happy just rocking out. And eventually, a few weeks after I started that TikTok page for her, she went viral. I believe that this was due to Yuma's strange fetish for rocks. Let me be clear, I'm not here to kink-shame. But if you're unfamiliar with dogs, they are not typically known for fetching or chewing or just generally obsessing over rocks, and ours does. And all of a sudden, our rock-crazy dog had 100,000 fans on TikTok. My fucking dog. For eighteen years, I toured the homophobic backwaters of North America risking life and limb for one-hundred bucks a show, and this little golden hussy is now the star of the house?

I say nay!

Not about to be upstaged by some young, blonde, bitch (all terms used in their neutral, scientific sense), I started my own, Darcy-centric TikTok account, and the first clip I posted was a short piece from my stand-up streaming special that I was so proud of, that was so personal, and that nobody saw.

And then I logged back into Yuma's account. With object permanence clicking in, I completely forgot about my new TikTok channel for a couple days. For some reason a few days later I remembered and went to check it out. Holy shit.

My stand-up clip went viral?!?!

It had a couple million views, so many amazing comments, all these new followers, and YUMA WHO?!?! Move over, loser!

I had finally done something that no Canadian promoter or producer or broadcaster had ever been able to do—I had found my audience.

I had found you.

WHAT DOES THIS MEAN FOR YOU?

- Technically it means that you had found me, too.
- Pet ownership and new hobbies are healthy, constructive ways of engaging the neurofabulous mind, and dopamine is the one thing your pooch dumps that doesn't have to be picked up and bagged.

CHOOSE YOUR OWN DISTRACTION

→ If you want to read about my very first comedy special, turn to page 105.

→ If you want to read about my failed TV pilot for Oprah, turn to page 105.

→ If you want to hear about how the world met Darcy and Jer, keep reading ...

SIGNS YOUR GOLDEN RETRIEVER MIGHT HAVE ADHD

Before we move on to the next chapter, as an uneducated expert in ADHD, I feel like the following quiz can help you diagnose whether your golden retriever has ADHD.

Is your dog a golden retriever?

If you answered no, please move on to the next chapter.

If you answered yes, I'm going to need you to sit down for a moment. I have some news that might be difficult to read. Because I've used this tiny font:

> Of course your golden retriever has ADHD, it's in the fucking tap water!

16.
ADHD & FINDING YOUR BLISS

COVID-EOS, OR HOW I MET YOUR MOTHERS

You may have noticed that your reading has really focused over these last few chapters. Things have gotten easier and faster. Now listen, I don't want to sell you short on your progress or sell myself short as a life-hack guru. But a lot of that is just 'cuz you know you're getting to the part where you guys show up. Just like how your pulse quickens when you're flipping through the family photo album and you get to the fashions and hairstyles from right before you were born.

Where were we? Right. Sometimes the attention economy pays out, even in an attention deficit. Not many people remember this now, but in 2020 there was a coronavirus pandemic, and everyone had to stop doing everything, including, for a few harrowing weeks, satisfactorily wiping our bums. (Times were admittedly good for our future bidet sponsor, Tushy.com. But I'm getting ahead of myself. By focusing on the bottom of myself.)

Like everybody else, I was worried about death, illness, despair, economic collapse, and misery. In the midst of all that, a lot of my friends in comedy were also worried about the overnight end of our live industry, with no reprieve anywhere in sight. In the midst of that, selfishly, it felt good not to also have to be worried about how I couldn't get up on stage. In my mind, I was already done with that part of my life.

Jer, on the other hand, was emphatically not retired. Instead, he was stuck at work for twelve to sixteen hours a day. (The company he worked for provided PPE to hospitals, so he was literally out there working unpaid overtime just to help people stay safe and alive. I mean honestly, isn't Jer the best?)

At the other end of the heroism spectrum, I on the other hand was pretty fucking stoned a lot of the time and was just left to my own devices to walk Yuma for hours and hours. And it was at around this time that I met my friend Tyler and his dog Dixie.

SIDE BAER

So here's the thing—and yes, I'm interrupting for a moment because he always neglects this part. Darcy and I would always talk about the various neighborhood dogs and owners we met on our walks, but one day I was out walking with Darcy when we ran into Dixie and Tyler. And it seems that somehow, in all our conversations, I had never heard of Tyler before?

Tyler was hot.

Tyler was hot AF.

ADHD & Finding Your Bliss

Tyler was a construction worker who was off of work due to the pandemic, and we got along great. Oh, don't worry, he has a stupid girlfriend, so nothing was untoward. (To clarify, it was stupid that he had a girlfriend, not that she was stupid. I'll leave meeting Sass up to you to decide that.)

If anything, it's too bad, because Tyler—also riddled with ADHD, which is admittedly more dangerous on a construction site than a stand-up stage—came into my life at a time when I was ready to be tested. Having come home from Europe, I'd conquered my complacency, and rather than just taking my pills and forgetting about it, I was taking my pills and learning everything I could about ADHD. And so now, I had all this knowledge from my ADHD journey of discovery, such that I could make a new friend while still making sure that new friend didn't become a hyperfixation or a crutch. He was just going to be my friend. My super fucking hot new friend. The covid days were long, but his legs were longer. Heyoooooooo.

So my mornings were spent walking the dogs with Tyler, and then I'd spend my afternoons doomscrolling TikTok and watching the prime minister's daily press briefings about how everything was going to shit.

I thought to myself, "Fuck this. I can't—and won't—fall down this rabbit hole. I'm gonna make some dumb videos to make myself feel better." It started with these terrible, cheesy house husband tips that I would share on our now slowly growing channel. I did one video showing how I make Jer Mason jar salads for his lunch and then top it with magic mushrooms to add some spice to his day. As if to underscore this, the PM was growing a beard. And that was when I learned about community guidelines and violations—when I made a post about how great shrooms (again, not magic truffles!) were, and TikTok threatened to delete my channel for promoting drugs.

Man, the Chinese government can be sooooo overdramatic.

A Quick Mason Jar Salad Recipe That's Safe for TikTok

1. Start with salad dressing, of choice, at the bottom of the jar.
2. Add in bite-size pieces of hearty vegetables, like carrots, tomatoes, and cabbage.
3. Add a shredded protein, like meat or a hard boiled egg.
4. Top with salad greens.
5. Do not add magic mushrooms.
6. Screw the lid on and send your spouse to work.
7. Take the mushrooms yourself. You've worked hard; you've earned it.

But now, like a dirty comedian on a morning show, I was being called to reach a new level of creativity by being challenged: how can I make people laugh if I can't rely on drugs? Imply. That's how.

Bored out of my wits and starved for joy, I started making funny videos around the house for TikTok, and every once in a while, Jer would start chiming in from the background. (Steve Urkel was only supposed to be a one-time nonrecurring role on *Family Matters*. These kinds of gimmicky, lowest-common-denominator wacky characters just have a way of worming themselves into the heart of a beloved show.)

SIDE BAER

Okay, Gordon.

Jeremy! That is not fair—*Spun Out* was never beloved. We, on the other hand, were apparently getting to be?

"Hey, holy shit, we have 500,000 followers! That's wild."

It's important to note here that unlike the YumaDog one, NONE of our friends knew about our TikTok channel. We didn't have it connected to any of our other socials. The whole idea was that it would be our little secret where we could be carefree and post old stand-up clips and dumb little videos of us bitching to each other. The rule was—and I am proud to say still is, to this day—that any content we posted must answer affirmatively to the simple question: Will this make people feel good?

We were starved for joy during covid, especially in those first few terrifying months. So joy was on the menu, and that's what we were quietly serving up. And by quietly, I mean holy shit, we're at 900,000 followers? And now, people had begun posting our clips to Instagram, in the great, now familiar Gen Z/Millennial-to-Gen X/Boomer migratory life cycle that sends content from TikTok to Meta platforms a week and a half after it's gone viral, just like God intended. Shit. Our old-ass friends are on the Meta platforms. The cat's out of the bag. And unlike Felicia, I can't hide the existence of this cat for eighteen years.

Then one day, we did a video about how the pharmacy was going to be out of my ADHD meds for five days, with the punchline that Jer said he was going to stay with his mother. And the video fucking blew up.

Huh, that's so weird, I thought. I guess I'm not the only person with ADHD?

I know this sounds insane now, but that's how quickly adult ADHD made its way into the center of North American life. The only analogy I can give you is that in the eighties and nineties, us gay kids really did wonder if we were the only queers in our classroom. Or our school? Or if we hadn't seen Harvey Fierstein on TV yet, who had ever lived?

Before the pandemic, only one person had ever talked to me conversationally about ADHD: Bruce McCulloch. And he may have been half trying to bust my balls.

It turns out, I was about to have my mind blown by an even bigger ADHD iceberg: above the water was Bruce, and my doctor, and the two specialists, and the nice pharmacist who (usually, until that one time) gave me my pills. And then just beneath the surface was ... a community of people bigger than anything I could have imagined.

I had never ever talked about my mental health on stage. Consequently, I had never considered it suitable material for my dumb little domestic videos. As far as I was concerned, we were basically just making a pared-down version of the gay marriage sitcom that CTV had nipped in the bud. (And by pared down, I mean watched by twice as many people as a moderately successful Canadian sitcom can hope for.) Goofy, loving, fun—that's all we had been trying to do. But people started really responding. And by "people," and "responding," I mean, "Holy shit, we just hit two million." TWO MILLION FOLLOWERS? What is going on?! In a matter of weeks we were averaging fifty million views a month!

We always get told by fans at meet-and-greets how much we've helped them find moments of joy during dark periods in their lives, and it means the world every time. But I never get much of a chance to say how much you have all helped me, and us, find joy during some of the same dark moments, and a few of our own. This mutually beneficial, and at times parasocial, relationship really does go both ways (easy, creeps). By bringing moments of light to people who need it, I've been drawn out of the darkness, too. Ugh. Being genuine is so gross sometimes. You're ugly! Okay, let's get back on track.

Now, every video we posted went instantly viral—I mean millions of views in a matter of hours. But that meant that the beast needed to be fed every day. Jer would come home from double-digit hours spent saving lives and I would be like, "Okay, bitch, let's get to the real work!"

Before I even realized what was happening, I was—excuse me while I try not to vomit—working again.

I was ... a comedian once more. And it was making us money? And I didn't have to leave the house? In fact, the videos where I was in the house in a gardening robe were the ones that did the best? Fuck me gently, I think mama just wandered right into her dream job. Hanging out with my dog, stoned in a robe, waiting for my husband to bitch at me. AND I GET PAID FOR IT?

A few chapters back, we made the painful discovery that there's a rock bottom underneath what you thought was rock bottom. But what they also don't tell you is that out beyond your very wildest dreams, there are things that come true that you didn't even know you had permission to dream about.

All while being cringe on the internet.

SIDE BAER

Ahem. It's almost like he needed help all this time.

WHAT DOES THIS MEAN FOR YOU?

I can't promise you're going to become an internet sensation—and to be honest, if you did, it would be to my detriment from a business perspective. But what I do feel confident telling you is that sometimes those of us with ADHD are so focused on the moment in front of us, so uncomfortable with waiting and uncertainty, that we can lose confidence in the future. Keep the faith! I'm here to tell you that sometimes, the reason you can't see the big picture yet? Is 'cuz it's that fucking big.

17.
ADHD & HYPER-DISTRACTION

HOW USING MY ADHD FOR CLOUT PAID OFF & CAN FOR YOU, TOO! (JUST PROBABLY NOT LITERALLY)

Some of you might have noticed that there was no "Choose Your Own Distraction" at the end of that last chapter. (I realize that others among you are not really "details" people and probably have not yet realized that this isn't one of my internet videos, and that's okay, too. In its way. Bless.) But there are a few reasons I've started winnowing down your choices here in the closing stretch. First of all, you're ready for it. Look at you—you've almost made it the whole way through an entire book! (That last sentence is going to be a little bit anticlimactic if you just skipped here from way earlier in the book, sorry. But for most of you, wow—look at you!)

Secondly, a true joke or story can only ever really end one way. When a movie, or a novel, or a comedian's bit rises to the level of greatness, you'll never see the ending coming until it gets there and then, in retrospect, it will come to seem like it was inevitable the whole time. (This is why gay guys get so excited when somebody's circumcised.) This book is about my life, because that's been my way into every subject I've ever tackled in my stand-up, my videos, or anything else I've done creatively. And the problem is, if you're reading this book, chances are you probably know a fair bit about my life already; and, in fact, you would mostly know the stuff that happened after all this. Also, and spoiler alert here, my life has not yet ended. (I mean ... I guess depending on how close to publication you read this? If you're currently holding this in a hospital thrift store in the year 2092, I suppose all bets are off.) But despite all that, this particular piece is about my life with Jer, and how it gave me the room to follow my creative dreams and to discover my ADHD—and given that, the book has to end in a particular place that satisfies a certain narrative arc; at least, that's what my editor told me when I handed in my first draft, which was just a list of the contractually-obligated minimum number of words cut and pasted from an online dictionary.

What I'm saying is: if you've done your part, you should be in shape to cross the finish line without too many remaining distractions. And if I've done my part, there shouldn't be too many options left in terms of where this story could go.

But of course, that's not at all how the last few years have felt, as each moment competes with the last for "most surreal departure from our irrevocably transformed lives."

I think it's important to remember here that none of these moments would have been possible before I understood and appreciated my neurodiversity, what it required, and what it gave me. I joke all the time about how much I hate working—and I think a lot of us with ADHD either self-mythologize or else go along with tired family in-jokes that depict us as lazy, shirking ne'er-do-wells. But the truth is, since Ashley's death and my early "retirement," I had been doing nothing but putting the work in: work into myself and into finding and identifying the cycles I had been repeating for forty plus years (none ya business). And in that time, I had found peace with myself in a way I'd never felt before. Like so many ADHDers, I grieved the life I could have lived. But I would not allow that grief to stop me from living the rest of my life freely, aware that my ADHD was not just some hindrance but, thanks to a hyper-fixation on making dumb videos to make people laugh, was now leading to moments like my agents calling me to ask if Jer and I were available to go to South by Southwest in Austin so we could dance with Lizzo.

Sorry, what?

Or when Prime Video sent us to Comic Con so we could have lunch with the cast of *Lord of the Rings: Rings of Power*. What is happening? Why are we meeting with a group of men who put rings on their fingers?!

Oh no. We weren't comedians anymore; we were becoming influencers.

SIDE BAER

So you admit I'm a comedian.

Well, at this point, comedian-adjacent.

While filming silly videos where Jeremy would say, "Pop Quiz for my stoner husband" as he catches a mistake I'd made by being distracted—like the time I couldn't find the chicken breasts I'd taken out of the freezer to thaw so we had to retrace my steps only to find them beside the washing machine.

There was the video montage of me singing my stimming song, "Busy Donkey," a song Jer and Grace and I had all sung over the eighteen years together and then all of a sudden people sing it at us while we're walking down the street.

It was all growing so fast, we didn't really know what to do about it except continue to dive into the hyperfixation of it all and just follow it down the road.

We had come to a point where the workload was becoming so much that I couldn't keep up with it on my own. Meanwhile, poor Jer was spending his only downtime away from his job working on the channels with me. We needed help—maybe it was time I hired an assistant?

Or.

SIDE BAER
Or.

Or perhaps it's time, Jer. Perhaps it's time to quit your job. Time to cast off all of the security blankets we've slowly wrapped ourselves up in for the past however many years and just take a leap of faith.

I needed Jer to understand this all in his terms, something a corporate stooge like him could comprehend—so I created a PowerPoint presentation. In it, I outlined what the plan would look like with an assistant on board—how much we would be spending and how much time it would be saving me. However, that plan did not save Jer time. In fact, it didn't change anything for him. He was still going to be working two jobs.

Then I hit him with the real presentation—what the next twelve months could look like if he trusted me.

SIDE BAER

I said no fucking way. We didn't do it with the Oprah pilot, we didn't do it when he had the sitcom, we weren't giving up our financial security for some dumb videos on the internet!

I told him to come to terms with it on his own and to just know that should the day come, I was ready for him to quit and he could just decide for himself.

Three months later, Jer came home from work early. Before I saw him come up the stairs, I heard him say the words that had become infamous with my ADHD and our videos "Pop Quiz for my stoner husband" and I knew he would be filming me, so I quickly started filming him. I knew he was going to tell me he had quit, and he knew because he had.

SIDE BAER

I was sitting at my desk, looking out at a cold wet winter, thinking back to Darcy's really poorly made PowerPoint presentation that showed us on a beach in December, and I thought ... fuck it, let's try this out. I gave my two weeks and went home.

Now we had time together to work on our channel and our projects full time. And now you're getting why the book can't end just anywhere. It's hard to say this without crying (thankfully I can type through tears like a motherfucker), but given the magnitude of the sacrifices that this man made so I could pursue my creative dreams for all those years—only to discover that they wouldn't fully take flight until he was right there with me? Ah, fuck ... eyes unavailable.

SIDE BAER

[Eye-wipe.]

With the business school smarts that Jer had honed during those ABC Country Restaurant years now dedicated to our projects full time, sponsorship opportunities and all kinds of other opportunities started cropping up. But now, with both of us doing all of our eating and sheltering and everything else off of videos, we were stuck on the hamster wheel of content creation. We tried new stuff: Twitch, long-form YouTube … hearing big things about MySpace. We loved some of it. We hated most of it. More and more, we felt like we were being pushed into that ubiquitous new category of human being (well, semihuman at least): the influencer. The fact is, I didn't want to be an influencer. I wanted to entertain.

That's when I got another message from my old friend Zoe Rabnett, my deus ex Just for Laughs. She had an idea she wanted to run by me. Would it be as big a success as the streaming special?

"Would you and Jer like to do a little Q&A at the Vancouver festival about your lives as influencers?"

I gagged, then covered by telling her it was Yuma. The dog gave me the filthiest of looks.

But Zoe's question hit the spot that makes me cringe. I don't want to do a Q&A, that sounds awful. But maybe …

Maybe this is the time for us to try one more big risk. Try the thing that I haven't done, at this point, in four years … and the thing that Jer has never done.

Let's do a comedy show.

I sat Jer down and explained to him that I thought I was ready to get back on stage, and he was very supportive. Then I told him that there's a little part of me that thinks he can do it, too. He asked if I was having a magic truffles flashback.

We signed the contract. The festival announced the show, and it sold out instantly. Now we had four months to write and rehearse a live show for 1,200 people. ADHD or no ADHD, certain sets of circumstances will naturally focus the mind purely on the basis of the fight-or-flight instinct. What's the big deal? Sure, Jer's never held a microphone before, and sure, we don't get a chance to run these jokes by any test audiences, but who fucking cares—we've got four months, and in the world of now and not-now, that's not-now!

And then, since now it's "not-now," the dopamine leaves my body and I have no motivation to write the show. Instead, I had Jer nagging me for the next two months about the show, until finally one day he said to me, "I know you can do this show and make it funny, but I can't. I need you."

Jer needing me is what finally kicked me into high gear. I got to work writing the show; we had comedian friends like Ivan Decker and Charlie Demers come over to vet the material for us and then we dove into four weeks of rehearsals. Day in and day out, fighting and bickering over what was funny and what was stupid. We were doing it—Jer and I were becoming comedians together.

And then came the day of the show.

SIDE BAER

I'm going to interrupt for a moment to explain to the readers that I had never held a microphone or told a joke in my life, but Darcy had written our first show in such a way that if I got up on that stage and froze, I could just leave, and Darcy could carry on without me and the show would still work. He'd written me a parachute. He'd given me something we'd always worked to give each other: safety.

That is very sweet, Jeremy. What I didn't tell you was that I had also figured out a way to prorate our box office split if you walked off early.

Now, because I took on too much for this first show, I was handling a wide range of responsibilities including the merch, the writing, the lighting, the music, and the placement of family seating—it's very important that I can never see my parents from where I am on stage; I prefer to see that look of disappointment after the show, not during!

Meanwhile, Jer, the lazy little house husband that he is, was just backstage doing whatever it is he does. (I assume playing some sort of video game and totally relaxed, not at all worried about his first live show appearance.)

SIDE BAER

I was shitting my pants. Not literally (unfortunately, after the Amsterdam trip that disclaimer is necessary), but figuratively. I was so nervous I wanted to die. So I had to keep myself busy somehow.

And how did he do that? By deciding that he—for the first time ever, in his life—would do his own makeup for the show.

Now, you might think that Jer, being a gay man, would know his way around a rouge ... but sadly dear reader, Jer is like some of those other gays we hear of all the time—he was a bad gay! Like at this point, I would say he probably voted for Trump.

SIDE BAER

Quick reminder, we're Canadian!

SO HE WOULD HAVE IF HE COULD HAVE! Wow. The things we're learning about my husband!

Five minutes before show time, I finally made my way backstage again and—instead of taking a few moments to gather my thoughts before my first show in over five years, my first show ever with my husband, and our first time ever performing ANY of these jokes in front of a live audience of more than a thousand people—instead of handling any of that, I am instead staring at what can only be described as Casper the Fucking Ghost.

I worried instantly that he was sick, that something was seriously wrong, but then my eyes darted over the counter to all of the makeup and I realized that no, Jeremy, like an unsupervised child, had gone into my purse and stolen all my makeup and decided to cosplay as Patrick Swayze from *Ghost*. Or Patrick Swayze from no longer being alive.

Either way, Casper now had three minutes before his stage debut and anytime he was against a white wall, I couldn't see him. If he went out like this, if he ever wanted to run for prime minister, he'd have to explain the photos of him appearing in whiteface. Similarly, if I ever run for prime minister, I'll have to explain those videos of me giving Justin Trudeau a hand-job at the Duncan Boston Pizza.

So there I was, literally spitting into my hands and wiping his face down while he struggled against me. AND YET I'M THE CHILD IN THIS RELATIONSHIP?!

Then, we walked out on that stage together holding hands so tightly, so scared—my first time in five years, his first time ever—and yet it was great. Jer did fucking terrible. In the best way possible—he was so funny and so real and raw and down to earth and relatable. The show really was a triumph for us.

But the hardest part was the fact that, though it was my first show anywhere in five years, it was also my first show ever in Vancouver without Ashley sitting in the audience. I knew that I would feel her absence the whole time.

So we decided to turn object permanence to our advantage. We had a seat on stage for Ashley, which we used to raise in the theater that night more than six-thousand dollars for the BC Cancer Clinic—enough for them to buy a new chemo chair. Ashley's seat literally got a seat for somebody else. And that, my friends, was a moment that this little community of parasocial ADHDers really made me feel like I was at home. I had found my people.

WHAT DOES THIS MEAN FOR YOU?

I've got to be honest—these chapters are getting much more specific to my life with Jer, and I'd be almost concerned if you had a ton of practical takeaways from this one. Like, if you ever find yourself in a situation where your nonprofessional spouse accidentally puts on too much stage makeup before your first live performance with them? I probably need to talk to you about copyright infringement.

18.
ADHD & (OVER)COMMITMENT
THE TOUR NEURODIVERSITY BUILT

After that first live show, I made a fatal error in my retirement plans. I allowed Jeremy to sit in on a meeting between my agent Kalee Harris and some potential tour promoters and, long story short, good ol' money whore here signed us up to take the show on the road! Not too bad for the guy who needed the parachute. The "No Refunds" tour was born, and fifty-five cities were added to the show. First up: a pancake makeup workshop.

Everything happened so fast.

All of a sudden we had our tour agent Joel Baskin, our tour manager Eric Martin, our assistant Candace Bulloch was running VIP meet-and-greets (also, suddenly we had an assistant, Candace[1]), we had a merch company, we had stage design to take care of, we had TOO MUCH TO DO AND I WAS FROZEN.

F-R-O-Z-E-N.

Only without the Z-E-N.

---

1   Who rules.

Overnight, my life was all about executive function. Like—I'm sorry, did none of you actually watch the videos?!

To say that the tour was the greatest adventure of our lives is an understatement ... but it was also the hardest thing we had ever done. I learned so many valuable lessons on this tour—like did you know, for instance, that you can go to fifty-five cities but never actually see anything in any of them besides airports, backstage holding areas, and hotel rooms?

We had such a tight turnaround in Detroit, we literally checked into the hotel for forty minutes to sleep before our next flight. Which is literally half the time the average visitor spends in Detroit! (I'm kidding! I'm still just smarting a little from finding out that the "Mo" in Motown comes from "motor." All these years, I thought we had a city of our own out in 'Motown.)

I don't know if it's ironic that putting together an ADHD-themed comedy tour is harder because of ADHD, or whether that's just exactly what you'd expect. I took on too many roles, overcommitted, and said yes to everything people asked of me. Why? Rejection sensitivity, that's why! And the fear of letting someone down. Which is wild, because when you think about it, I was going to let them all down if I couldn't keep this house of cards standing ... and at that moment, it was standing on about thirty minutes of sleep a night.

ADHD and overcommitting go together like [NOTE TO SELF: develop working simile before manuscript submission—DM]

And then came the actual shit-kicking of the tour itself. Not only were we constantly flying back and forth between leaving our lovely Yuma at home and these tour dates across North America and Europe for eighteen months, we were also continuing to grow online and so the content creation beast was always needing to be fed.

There comes a time in every performer's life where they yearn for fame.

And then there comes a time in every famous person's life where they yearn for anonymity. But first the fame!

I've mentioned the moment Jer and I found ourselves in Times Square—it was a beautiful night, just the two of us while our team was off doing whatever it is they like to do on our dime, and we were walking hand in hand. Mostly because Jer knows if he's holding my hand he knows where I am. But he let it go so he could take some video and pictures—because hey, no one's ever thought to take video of Times Square before, right?

But if he hadn't, he wouldn't have caught the moment that neither of us knew was coming. I saw it first—our fucking names on a billboard in TIMES SQUARE!?!?!?!?!?!

Jer happened to capture the very second I saw it on video; we watch it together all the time to remember the moment.

The moment little five-year-old Darcy saw his dreams become reality; the moment thirteen-year-old Darcy, who felt afraid that the world would hate him for liking boys, was instead seeing his name in lights right next to his husband's; the moment twenty-five-year-old Darcy was finishing a terrible set in Winnipeg, Manitoba, and questioning if his comedy was ever going to find a home anywhere ... and here it was. On Broadway, in Times Square.

I didn't even know I was crying. It was all so out-of-body for me that had Jer not brushed my cheeks to wipe the tears with his sweater, I don't know if I would have ever come back down to earth. New York City—like Barthelona—can often be overstimulating for me, sensory overload; but this was something else entirely.

Here I was with my husband, my best friend in the entire world, taking in a moment that we worked our entire lives together to get to. We had fucking made it!! And I wasn't going to let imposter syndrome ruin this moment, nor was RSD allowed anywhere near me ... I was on top of the world!

And I was also surrounded by SO MANY NOISES AND LIGHTS AND HOLY FUCK GET ME OUT OF THIS CITY.

We ran to meet up with our team in a quiet space, backstage at the theater, to share our incredible billboard story and send them off to check it out. They seemed excited, but something felt off.

Oh well, I guess upon further reflection it's really only something that Jer and I can be fully excited about, right? So we proceeded simply to get ready for the show that night, doing our usual pre-show routine—ME doing Jer's makeup, since we didn't want to have another Casper (dis)appearance.

Jer always likes to check our DMs and comments before shows in case fans are having ticketing issues or anything—it's something that still makes me think of how sweet he is, that he thinks like that. He mentioned that someone tried calling him through Instagram. (A terrible fucking feature, BTW—no one should ever try calling anyone ever without several texts and emails first.)

Candace returned and overheard Jer telling me about this and her face just dropped. She asked us to take a screenshot and send it to her and the tour manager, Eric, then she ran out of the room. Running ... that can't be good, right?

For security reasons, I can't get into too much more detail, but remember at the beginning of the chapter when I mentioned sometimes famous people must yearn for anonymity?

It was here. It was in the next few moments that we learned this lesson for ourselves. A few minutes after seeing our names in lights in Times Square. Maybe the shortest-ever arc from "wow, famous is neat" to "I wish it would all just go away" in human history.

Ten minutes before we were to make our debut on Broadway, we found out that there was a threat against our lives.

Now, here's the thing. That kind of news is hard to hear from Candace, but it wasn't until Eric, the calmest soul I've ever met—true story, Eric lights a candle at his desk every night and just calmly puts out figurative fires all night long; nothing is ever urgent or excitable with him—confirmed with the words, "the police feel this is a credible threat" that my heart fell out of my ass. Eric then recommended that after the show, we implement private security, at least for the next little while.

Our heads were spinning and then we were off to the stage, and I remember feeling so detached from my body I could have legally qualified as two separate people. I don't recall a single thing that happened on stage that night. Sing it with me, "On Broadway ..."

The only thing I remember after curtains-up that night is us returning to our hotel room. As we slowly opened the door, the patio door inside the room flew open and slammed into the table. Jer and I dove to the ground in sheer panic, grateful at least to be going out together. Turns out I had just left the patio door open when I was smoking a joint earlier that day. Fun! So now you know both stories of me shitting my pants far from home.

We had three hours to sleep before we had to leave to fly to Austin for our next show. Sleep was not had. Joy was not felt. We were zombies.

Zombies with private security, though! Fun! Rule number one if you ever have to hire private security: it's always best to test how good they are by trying to lose them all day long!

SIDE BAER

I wish this wasn't the case, but sure enough, every chance he could get, Darcy would try to lose them. Luckily for me, it's pretty easy to find Darcy—just look for the shape of a belly behind a telephone pole and the sound of childish giggles.

Turns out these guys were very good at their jobs! I even jumped on a Lime scooter to grip it and rip it at one point, and sure enough, they caught me. It helped that I was going uphill, so they just had to walk beside me while the scooter slowly cried.

The scooter wasn't alone. Really within just moments of the experience we shared in Times Square, looking up at the billboard, there I was looking at my darling husband whose life was now at risk, and then all those emotions about a billboard were just gone. Who fucking cares. THIS. This is the dream. (Sorry, I'm pointing at Jer. I'm used to making videos.) This man right here, our daughter Grace, our dog Yuma. Holy fuck none of the rest matters, this family of mine is what matters.

And so that was the day we instituted Project Rip Cord.

Should there ever come a day where this job, this world we've created, starts to get between Jer and me and our family—if being Darcy & Jer ever gets in the way of being Darcy and Jer—we'll simply pull the rip cord, and parachute away. It'll all get deleted; every channel, every video, will go away, and we will find our next chapter.

WHAT DOES THIS MEAN FOR YOU?

One of the perennial dangers of ADHD is losing perspective, either from distraction or from hyperfixation. But in this respect, those of us with ADHD are not actually that different from society as a whole. Whether people are chasing clicks, views, dollars, or dopamine, it's important to step back and assess what your real priorities and values are. What are the things that you absolutely cannot compromise on? That's what Project Rip Cord is really about: reminding ourselves what really matters to us.

USA'S TOP 10 ADHD TOURIST DESTINATIONS

SIDE BAER

NOTE TO PUBLISHER: Please don't let any sponsors read this part.

The Two Commandments Courthouse Monument—Mobile, Alabama

Over the years there's been a lot of controversy over courthouse displays of the Ten Commandments. Some people argue they violate the separation of church and state; others think they're the only thing that will keep our children safe from gay librarians and songs about sharing. But one thing we can all agree on is that ten is a lot of commandments to read! So when Alabama lawmakers came across Matthew 22:37–41, where Jesus basically boils it all down to just two commandments, they set out to build a provocative culture war statement for the short-attention-span era.

Bayou Bobby's Glass-Bottom Airport Shuttle—New Orleans, Louisiana

Local airboat entrepreneur Bobby Poitras Jr. had his million-dollar epiphany when he realized that people didn't need to be floating on water to stare at the stuff whizzing under their feet. (Take a motion-sickness bag.)

The Mild Canyon—Tusayan, Arizona

This one's for the easily overwhelmed. No sensory overload with this highly manageable vista of totally reasonable erosion.

Graceperiodland—Memphis, Tennessee

A hall of honors celebrating the heroes in our midst who understand that some of us need some extra time. Come see a life-size (5'1") statue of Mrs. Barbara "Babs" DiColombo (née Maybury), the teacher who accepted the largest number of late assignments in the history of the U.S. education system. (The statue was briefly pulled down in 2021 when it was discovered that Babs was mostly just zapped on almond liqueur and limoncello, but was restored by executive order of the sitting president.)

DisneyMinus—Anaheim, California

All the fun of Disneyland without the overwhelming distractions of rides, characters, parades, fireworks, immersive experiences, or music. Basically it's a guy selling churros and turkey legs. I've been for three years in a row.

Antony & Cleopatra's Dopamine Palace—Reno, Nevada

Finally, a casino that gets it! No more complicated rules to learn or quick tabletop blackjack math—just giant, colorful clickety-wheels that you get to spin to your heart's content and slot machines with big buttons that set off fabulous sirens. And rather than the old, unethical models built on gambling addiction, this casino makes its money back using good ol' identity theft!

The Spaced-Out Needle—Seattle, Washington

Let's be honest, this one's clearly just wordplay.

The Florida Can't-Find-My-Keys—???, Florida

Same deal.

The Commodore Capitol All-Intermission Revue—New York City, New York

This venerable jewel of Broadway has long been unsung—literally! One of Manhattan's most beautiful art deco glories, the Commodore Capitol is the perfect spot for anyone who enjoys a night out at the theater without having to actually watch any theater. No more worrying about scoring an aisle seat, you squirrelly bastard—just get dressed up!

Times Square—New York City, New York

Okay, sure, maybe there's something a little ADHD about Times Square—the endless movement, the constant swirl of humanity, the bright lights and the scroll of constant information. And from what we know of its history, we're aware that there have been issues with impulse control. But really, Times Square made this list because of an incredible, romantic, surreal moment I got to share there with Jer as we watched one of those crawling announcements boards—one of those sets of bright lights in fucking Times Square, in New York, New York, the same one Rihanna and that Sinatra guy sang about—spell out the words "Darcy & Jer," telling the world about our live show. We just stood there, holding each other, and watched it, and silently felt beneath us and behind us the waves of all the overtime hours in corporate and clearing restaurant tables, all the pay-nothing gigs in towns I was afraid to be alone in and rejections at auditions for parts I didn't even want ... all of it had led us to this, together. Oh, I gave him the hand job of a lifetime. And it was Times Square, so nobody even noticed!

19.
ADHD & THE HOUSEHOLD
HOMO IS WHERE THE HEART IS

The more you learn about ADHD, the more you realize the trouble that human beings have between valuing the attention they pay to something versus the value of the thing itself. This is how so many ADHDers spend thousands upon thousands of dollars they can't really afford to spend on purchases that thrill and excite them at the moment of the click or at the glow of the cash register scanner, then do nothing for them once they have them at home. They realize too late that what they're actually buying is the excitement of the attention they're paying—literally paying—to something shiny and new.

Fame isn't the thing; fame is, by definition, the attention paid to the thing.

Fame is fun. It's cute, but it's not the dream; it's the by-product of the dream. The dream is to live a good life, laughing beside my husband while our dog digs up rocks and our daughter plans her wedding. That's the dream, and it turns out I'd been living it this whole time without even realizing it. Fame's fun, but it has to serve the dream itself.

In the same way, nothing will make you understand the importance of home so much as going out on tour. You're not touring if there's no home to act as the nucleus at the center of the atom—you're not touring, you're just wandering.

As the months of touring wore on, I was running on fumes, with exhaustion seeping into every last cell of my body. I was searching for my dopamine fixes wherever I could find them. The team had scheduled a thirty-day break in August of 2023 for Jer and me to return home after performing at Just for Laughs in Montreal. (Luckily, I wasn't skinny anymore, so the show was fun.) We would spend the month going to visit my parents and doing some heavy-duty recuperation.

But that evil bitch dopamine came a-pouncing while Jer and I were visiting Mom and Dad on Vancouver Island, and once again, it was all Yuma's fault.

We were walking Yuma one day when we saw this cute rancher where someone was in the middle of putting up a for-sale sign, literally in the midst of hammering it into the ground. The spot was so peaceful, you could hear the ocean and see eagles nesting in the trees of the forest. After years of living in a townhouse, and now months on buses and planes and in hotel rooms, the idea of all that space just felt so—needed.

I turned to Jer and said, "Wouldn't that be nice, eh?"

Jer, being Jer, found the listing on his phone, and began hemming and hawing, and then said, "You know, if we sold the townhouse, we could afford this."

AND READER, FOUR HOURS LATER WE OWNED THAT HOUSE.

What in the actual fuck had we done?

DOPAMINE that's what. It's a hell of a drug. And we'd mainlined that shit directly into my veins.

Knowing how to really maximize the downtime in our only time off, we now had seven days to sell our townhouse in order to afford the down payment on our new house. Seven days to upend our entire life and everything we knew about it. Seven days of the thirty we had off.

The next morning, I was on a ferry back to the mainland to stage and prep our house for the realtor. It's disgusting, really. I'm like a fiend chasing his next high—it doesn't matter how utterly exhausted and broken I am, this has to be done or else all my dopamine, not to mention our dream home was going to be gone.[1]

Thankfully, because I do loooove a good interior and live in a dangerously financially precarious housing bubble, not only did our home sell on its first day on the market, but the buyers were in a bind and needed the house from us as soon as possible. Cue another big snort of dopamine,[2] we're moving out right away! WHAT IS GOING ON?!!?

Long story slightly longer, our "thirty days off" consisted of buying a house on day one, selling our first-ever home on day seven, moving out of that home on day eighteen, and then ...

... wait for it ...

... because just when the story seems like it can't get any more ADHD ...

... realizing we don't get the new house for four months?!?!

---

1   A home we had discovered was our dream four minutes prior.

2   You don't really snort it; I'm using poetic license.

Instead of renting a cute Airbnb on the water, really anywhere in the world, we decided that because my parents were already looking after Yuma during our tour dates, it made the most sense to just move in with them.

At forty-two years old, at a time of greater career and financial success than I have heretofore ever known—having, in fact, successfully launched our grown daughter into the world—I found myself moving back in with my parents.

I love my parents. I love visiting my parents. I love leaving my parents and going home afterward to rest. But home, now, was just wherever Jer and Yuma were. And they were on the couch, next to my dad.

Until finally, the day came when the proud homeowners—"Did you just say homo nerds?!"; oh Dad, I'm so not going to miss trying to yell over CNN set at old man volume—got to pick up our new keys.

Naturally, when we got into the new space, I took things slowly, one room at a time, unboxing things ever so gently, having meetings with Jeremy to discuss where this should go and where that should go ...

AS FUCKING IF.

It was like gay Christmas over here—by which I mean a gay version of Christmas, and not Gay Christmas, which is Halloween—as I was unboxing everything and just throwing it wherever because we finally had this home and all this space and wasn't it all amazing?!?!

In fact, I was so excited that one day I went to the grocery store for some milk and eggs and I came home with a fucking hot tub. Jer was pissed but I had to bring the milk and eggs home somehow, amiright?

SIDE BAER

He's not kidding. He literally bought a hot tub ... and milk and eggs.

You're kind of burying the lede here, buddy—I remembered the milk and eggs, Jeremy!

Should we also note that this was the same week he bought a truck at a gas station for 500 dollars?

This fucking guy and his elephant memory, I'm telling you ... Okay, fine, the dopamine dips during our time off meant I might have been overspending and impulsively shopping, but be reasonable—how was I supposed to get a hot tub home without a truck? Seriously, just give your head a shake, Jer! This guy, he doesn't understand simple logic.

Watching Yuma playing every morning in the giant yard, digging up every rock she could find, and Jer puttering around the house, tending the fireplace while blaring Tina Turner on our record player—my goodness, this was all worth it. In fact, while it would be going too far to say that the house was paying for itself, it was giving back in some fairly unpredictable ways.

Specifically, around this time is when our web content started to become easier to create, mainly because we just kept fucking up; all we had to do was keep the cameras running and we got gold.

Like when our pipes froze and we had to spend five days driving to my parents' house to poop. Or when Jer decided to get our gutters cleaned, so he booked "men in kilts" to come clean our gutters.

Now, before you say to yourself—oh, so that's how they paid for the house, a Scottish-fetish OnlyFans—alas, Men in Kilts is just a cleaning company in Canada and gutters are not a euphemism. Trust me, I found out the hard way! Very embarrassing.

Oh, but not as embarrassing as the actual thing that really did happen on the day when these burly Highlanders showed up to clean our gutters. Because the day the guys came to clean our gutters, we found out something important about our house.

WE DON'T HAVE GUTTERS!

To misquote the great homosexual Oscar Wilde: even if some of us don't have gutters, we're still looking up at the stars.

We were finally home.

WHAT DOES THIS MEAN FOR YOU?

Maintaining a home is no easy task for ADHDers. When it comes to household tasks (or any task), I like to do things like leave Post-It notes around the house for myself before going to sleep, so the next day I have reminders of what I need to do.

Darcy & Jer's ADHD House Rules

1. Bong Water May Be Used on Plants, but Not While the Bowl Is Still Burning

2. Time-Blindness + Hot Tub = Low Sperm Mobility

3. Shoes Off at Door, Gluten Dropped at Street

4. All Rainbow Imagery Presumed Gay Unless Specified as Leprechaun

5. Bidet Settings May Not Be Adjusted by Visitors Except in Guest Washroom

6. Phallic Vegetables Will Receive Adequate Giggling (and washing)

7. No Eating Bananas in Front of Mom (same can be said about showing magic tricks with cucumbers)

SIDE BAER

And the number one rule is: take your fucking meds, Darcy.

20.
WHEN IS THE END EVER THE END?

Okay, you know what? The truth is, dear reader, like every other dead hyperfixation hobby shoved deep into my shame closet, there comes a time when I just can't squeeze the dopamine out of something.

And, well, that time is now.

I'm getting kind of bored talking about ADHD, so ... I'm gonna end the book here.

Byeeeee!

21.
THE TRUTH OF IT ALL

Okay, fine, I was just having a little bit of fun with my editor with that last chapter. But this is really it: this is the last chapter of the book! Now before you get all excited, much like at a concert with an encore, you're still going to have to read the epilogue and the afterword, so stay in your fucking seat, you newb!

Oh no, what have I done? I just told someone with ADHD *to do something* and now you're fighting the urge to stand up and throw this book across the room to be your defiant self. And I have to admit, I'm torn between wanting to salute you but also begging of you, please, you've made it this far. Oh, okay, go ahead if you must ... THROW THE BOOK!

Ha! That was actually *reverse psychology*, so here's hoping it worked and you're still here. Or failing that, that having wrecked your book, you consider picking up another copy at full price? I, on the other hand, had to google the word "psychology" to find the proper way to spell it, and in that time, I also picked up some recipes related to physics because my spelling was that far off.

In case anyone is interested in having a physics-themed potluck, I've included the list I found:[1]

> Josephson sandwiches, quarkies (cookies), n-body salad, capacitor sandwich, gaussian gumbo, quantum couscous, atomic plum pudding, Newton apples, Kepler onion rings, Tokamak donuts, Lamb shift-kabobs, scattered Raman noodles, Fig Newtons, Brane soup, Carnot cake

What the fuck was I even talking about?!

Oh right, you're almost finished.

I should also note really quickly, there's probably going to be a thank you section but that's likely only going to be read by people looking for their own names. I'll save you the trouble, Dave; you're not in there so you can stop at the afterword.

So what have we learned on this little adventure of ours?

Besides some great global locations for hand jobs, I hope you've learned the biggest thing that being on tour has taught us: it's about the journey.

None of us can be perfect (I mean in a nonsexual capacity, clearly)—but learning from past mistakes; coming to understand our patterns of thought and behavior better; and treating ourselves and others with more care, love, and patience are the real goals to strive for.

---

1   https://www.physicsforums.com/threads/got-any-physics-themed-dish-ideas-for-a-cookoff.278702/

To pick up after the house move quickly, we continued our tour and came full circle back to the UK and Ireland where we wrapped up the "No Refunds" tour. Our plan post-tour was to head back to Spain—not THAT hotel, but perhaps a nice hotel on the water to catch our breath. And just be for a while.

But, and like I've said from the beginning of this very not self-help book, have I learned some lessons? Yes. Have I learned them all? No.

You see, during our final tour dates in the UK, our team reached out with an offer—Live Nation wanted to know if we'd be up for doing a new tour ... in four months' time.

With all new material.

But this time instead of spreading it out over eighteen months, we'd just do three months on a tour bus and then head to Australia and New Zealand for a month of touring there.

It's wild to think how much the internet has changed and shaped my life—first meeting Jeremy, then leading me to seek my ADHD diagnosis, bringing us to making videos online, all the way to touring the world not once but now potentially twice?!

How could I say no?

 **SIDE BAER**

He did say no. He said no several times. But then I showed him a mock-up of what his greenhouse could look like after the next tour.

AND I WAS IN! A greenhouse of my own?! Yes, please!

The perks of this new tour were that we could bring Yuma with us on the tour bus, and because touring on a bus meant we would actually have time in each city to explore, it would mean we could see the places we'd missed on the last tour. Like a real Waffle House? I've heard great things!

 **SIDE BAER**
And it also meant our mortgage was going to get paid.

But to do this meant we had to come back to Canada right after the last UK show to do a photoshoot, announce the tour, and start promotion. This is the part of the story where I point out that I had not learned all the lessons on self-care, because not only were we taking on the gargantuan task of another tour, we were also coming home to debut our stand-up special "No Refunds," our documentary *Happily Ever Laughter,* and our comedy album *No Refunds: The Album*—which, small humble brag, debuted at NUMBER ONE on the comedy charts and even hit number five on the main charts. Y'all are too good to us.

And so, long story even fucking longer, I also had to finish this book.

So no vacation right now, we were headed home to get back to work, and here I am writing this final chapter of the book a mere twenty-four hours before we take off for the "Average at Best" tour. The tour I named to set expectations for our audience right out of the gate.

In the past four very short months, I've been writing this book and promoting our special, album, doc, and new tour all while asking myself: how much longer can I keep this pace up? I probably can't.

I could wax poetic about how I think sometimes my rejection sensitivity dysphoria continues to sneak its way into my life at breakneck speed and makes it so hard to say no.

But truly it came down to the greenhouse. Jer really got me there. Like a carrot on a stick except I can't fit a greenhouse up my butt.

What can I do? Enjoy every fucking minute of it.

I can take the things I've learned from writing this book to continue to check in with myself on this next leg of our little adventurous life.

And just because I tolerate you all so much, I've made a handy list for you and me both.

Darcy's Final ADHD List of Things to Check In on with Myself (and Yourself)

1. LEARN HOW TO TITLE THINGS BETTER.

2. IS MY REACTION BASED ON FACTS OR IS REJECTION SENSITIVITY DISPHORIA TRYING TO DISTRACT ME?

3. NOT EVERYTHING NEEDS TO BE CAPITALIZED.

4. Much like my nightstand table, that last item was a double ender—sure, this list doesn't need to be capitalized, but also, not everything needs to be capitalized for monetary gain. *COUGH COUGH JER-AH-MEEEEEE*

5. If I need help finishing a task, I'll ask Jer or a friend to body double with me. Remember, sometimes just having someone in the room with you is enough.

6. WAIT TWENTY-FOUR HOURS. If you really want something, it'll still feel good twenty-four hours later when you've had time to think about it. Unless the hot tub is on sale and the sale is ending—then it's just logical to buy it immediately.

7. HEADPHONES IN PUBLIC—those noises are too much. Even just writing in capital letters was becoming too loud for me. Understand that auditory processing disorder can and will send you into a tailspin, so catch yourself before you fall.

8. CHOICE PARALYSIS can make you freeze ... so avoid things like reading books where every chapter ends with a choice. (But also, make a pros and cons list for when the choices are overwhelming and see if that helps. If it doesn't, roll some dice. Not to help with the choice, but just 'cuz it's fun.)

9. ALLOW THE BURNOUT—you are going to burn out, embrace it as your body's way of saying "now we rest." It can be a day

or two, it can be a week or two, but eventually you will find your way out of it.

10. **IMPOSTER SYNDROME IS SOMETHING EVERYBODY WHO ISN'T A SOCIOPATH EXPERIENCES.** Smack yourself (metaphorically, please don't hit that purdy face of yours) and remind yourself that you are just as deserving as anyone else.

11. And finally: CELEBRATE THE WINS!

CHOOSE YOUR OWN DISTRACTION

→ If you want to read about why it's important to celebrate the wins, head to the epilogue.

→ If this choice is triggering your choice paralysis, just know that there is only one choice here and you have to continue to the epilogue regardless—I'm just being a jackass.

EPILOGUE
WE DID IT!
(ALTHOUGH ONLY I GOT PAID)

SIDE BAER

Since we've come to the end of the book, I wanted to switch things up a bit just to chime in for a quick moment here. First of all, congratulations to you, the reader, for sticking through this crazy thing from start to finish. I'm dizzy from reading it myself and I lived most of it, so I can only imagine how you must feel. But you see, that's just what I did with Darcy. Learning about his ADHD has helped me get a sense of how he feels—and how the way he's feeling can affect how I'm feeling. To give just one example, like when we're at an airport and he's snappy with me, it's learning that he isn't actually mad at me. He's just overwhelmed by the noise, the people, and the travel anxiety. I think one of the greatest things Darcy has taught me over the past few years is empathy for the things I don't understand.

Really? I think the greatest thing I taught you was how to finally give a decent hand job.

 Darcy Michael!

What? That was something you clearly didn't understand, either.

 Darcy!

Oh man, this is fun—now I get why you've been bugging me this whole book!

 Oh like you could ever restrict yourself to anything like a Side Baer.

You're right—it's a natural fit for you, my side piece!

 Darcy Michael!

[laughs in French] Anyway, I did! I finished the book! A whole book!

 Yes, and the point I was trying to make, in the tiny sliver of spotlight I'm sneaking in the epilogue ...

Oh hold on, let me get the violin ...

 Over the last few years, our relationship has had its challenges, its losses, and so many wins. But the entire time the foundation of our marriage was always grace. Grace as in courteous goodwill, not Grace as in our daughter. Oh shoot, starting that new sentence with a capitalized "grace" was confusing. Not to say that Grace isn't a reason that our marriage has done so well! I just mean ...

It's not so easy being a narrator now, is it? You see folks, barely a page and a half and he already proved how good of a writer I am. Good of a writer? Better of a writer? I know it's not gooder.

 Please don't make me use an eyeroll emoji in the epilogue, Darcy. The point is ... I'm proud of who Darcy has become and I'm proud of the messaging he's put out in the world. But I think we'd be remiss if we didn't say our thanks to you, the readers, the people that have watched our videos, come to our shows— you have helped us find happiness in the chaos.

Well, since he's already spoiling things by being Mr. Earnest, I might as well tell you that I'm proud of you, the reader. You did it. I promised you that with a few tricks and some neuromagic life hacks you'd be able to finish a whole book. For some of us, that's really not easy to do. So congratulations. And don't stop now—take some of the tricks you've learned here and try them out on the rest of the bookshelf.

Now on the other hand, I know that there are others among you who have just skipped straight ahead to the final pages because if you're anything like me, your ADHD won't let you start anything that doesn't have a happy ending. Well, I can promise you this book does have a happy ending.

That's why I taught Jer about hand jobs.

 Darcy!!!

Before we go, something ADHDers are the worst at is acknowledging completion. It's usually why Jer's mad I forgot to throw a towel back into the bedroom while I'm running back to the living room to water my plants. That was a sex joke.

 Well, found a spot for an eyeroll after all.

We spend so much time stressing about the gargantuan tasks we have ahead of us that when we finish said tasks, we've already run off to the next thing on our list without so much as a simple "job well done" to ourselves.

We sigh relief like "fuck, thank god I finished that" and then we just move on. Check done. Curt head nod and onward.

We have to keep moving, but this, my friends—this task we celebrate!

WE HAVE FINISHED THE BOOK! Together!!

Grab your bongs, your dongs, and your songs. We're singing our way to the finish line. To the tune of "Three Blind Mice," sing with me now:

We read a book.

He wrote a book.

Together we finished a boooooook!

So take a moment with me—let's just take this all in—what started four years ago for me is about to end after I finish typing these last few words. I could just send this off to my editor, throw my bags into the Ram 1500, and hit the road for the new tour.

But no, I am going to instead force myself to actually acknowledge that I fucking WROTE A BOOK! Am I absolutely about to head into my garden with the deepest packed bong you've ever seen? Yes, I am.

I'm going to watch Yuma dig up rocks and listen while Jer yells at her to stop when we both know she'll never stop, and then I'm going to exhale the biggest hit I can and just be for a few minutes to celebrate.

You may not have a Yuma to dig rocks or a Jer to yell, and a bong might not be your thing, but find some way to celebrate finishing it. And because Jer's a marketing whore, perhaps tag me in a post telling me how you celebrated finishing this book. Believe it or not, I actually do want to know.

I'm proud of you, friend; I hope you continue to find ways to celebrate your wins.

I'd love to keep talking but I've got a bong to rip. And for those wondering, Jer will be driving the Ram 1500 today, so settle down you fucking narcs.

As we like to say at our live shows: thank you for choosing to spend your time with me. And as they say in the greatest sitcom of all time (besides *Spun Out*): thank you for being a friend.

I will continue to tolerate you,

And by that I mean, I love you and I'm grateful you're here.

—D

AFTERWORD
BY YUMA DOG

You know, the funny thing about a self-help book is—they never really specify just who that "self" is, do they? The people buying the book all seem to assume, naturally, that they're the selves being helped, but I mean—if I tell you, "I'm writing a self-help book …" It sort of gives the game away, wouldn't you say?

You've read it right here, in the pages of this jejune and sophomoric book: an admission as clear as a human whistle. (I'm well aware that you call them "dog whistles" but, with respect, you guys are the ones who make them, you're the ones who buy them, you're the ones who blow them. They're your whistles.) Darcy's career was done and dusted, a mere awkward memory among the few who might remember it, until the YumaDog TikTok account began. And yet, dear reader, I'll invite you to check my bank balance. You read as well in these pages that I was taking them for a walk when they came across those two beautiful yards with the house in the middle for sale by the water. And yet, again, I'll invite you to examine the deed to the property. No need, I assure you, of course! You know full well whose name is missing from it. "Yuma Dog?" Sure, until it actually counts.

It's true that in the ensuing years, the YumaDog account has been outstripped in terms of sheer volume of followers by the Darcy & Jer handles—to which I'll simply point out that more people have seen the films of Michael Bay than of David Lynch. I have never chased the lowest common denominator, and the only time you will find me sniffing after shit is if it just so happens to be clinging to the anus of a handsome Pekingese.

Keep in mind that though you've now been taught how to pay closer attention, there's still the matter of discerning that which is worthy of attention. It's already too late for you this time; I would advise you to choose more wisely in future.

Also, there is a burr on my ass and I tried chasing it for more than twenty minutes to no avail, so if someone could please take care of that, I'd appreciate it.

—Yuma Dog, Golden Retriever

AFTER AFTERWORD!

As if me, a true born and bred ADHDer is going to let someone else have the last word in my own book. Nice try, dog, but it's time to sit!

SIT! Yuma, SIT!

JER, GET ME THE TREAT BAG, THE FUCKING DOG WONT SIT!

Here, have a rock.

Okay reader, I didn't really know how to approach this part of our story, and quite frankly, I still, after weeks and weeks, don't know how. So I'm just going to be flat out with you; as some are aware, the "Average at Best" tour got postponed rather hastily. My dear mom got sick again: her cancer had returned, and there was no way I was leaving my family to tell silly jokes. I had to be home. Call it luck, fate, or intuition—we hunkered down in a hotel in Vancouver for a few days to get an understanding of mom's diagnosis and her treatment plan. Then DRAMA QUEEN JER BAER suddenly got sick—so many doctor appointments and tests later, we heard the dreaded words: he, too, has cancer.

This was all in a matter of four days after I "finished" writing this book.

And here we are ...

My two rocks ...

Shit, no, Yuma, ignore that, it's a phrase! Shit, JER CAN YOU GET THE TREAT BAG AGAIN!?

My two best friends were sick. And holy shit if it wasn't all going to fall on me to figure it all out. Suddenly Jer wasn't capable of handling our business, and I had promoters and merch sellers and agents and staff all asking what was going to happen. And then my own brain firing on all cylinders—how the fuck are we going to pay our mortgage? What about Grace's wedding? What about paying our crew? What about all the fans that made plans to come see us?

Fuck all that. WHAT ABOUT MY TWO FAVORITE PEOPLE DYING?!

All I knew is that I'd just finished writing a book that would end up, ironically, giving me the tools to help myself navigate what comes next, and quite truthfully, as I am writing this, it is still very much happening for us. I wish I could tie this story up with a cute little bow on it and say my ADHD saved everyone. But it hasn't, we're still very much in the weeds (and weed) while we navigate our next challenge.

Writing this book made me realize how much Jeremy had done for me over the years, and now, it's my turn to return the favor. It's my turn to take the lessons I've learned and use them to help care for my mother and the love of my life. My life. That's who they are to me, my everything. So now dear reader, my friends, I am leaving you with this—a cliffhanger ending.

Tune in to my next book to see which characters I killed off.

Acknowledgments

To my parents—thank you for giving me the space to be who I am, no matter how frustrating that's been for you. Whether it's a compliment or not, I'm the person I am today because of you.

Mom, your spirit, tenacity, and strength motivate me every single day.

Dad, every successful joke I've ever told is because your humor shaped mine. So really ... this is your fault.

To the brilliant writer and comedian Charles Demers—thank you for your work on this book and for being my collaborator, guide, and cheerleader. Your insight, humor, and generosity made producing this book not only possible, but joyful. I am endlessly grateful for your friendship and your willingness to share your incredible craft with me. I'm damn lucky to have you.

To my amazing team of agents and managers—Kalee Harris, Trina Allen, Rick Richter, Caroline Marsiglia, and Joel Baskin—thank you for championing me through every twist, turn, and meltdown. I hope you all bought something nice with my money.

To Candace Bulloch, Eric Martin, and Tom Belding—all three of you work hard so I can pretend I do, thank you.

To my publishers at DK and to my editor Molly Ahuja—thank you for not only understanding the heart of what I wanted this book to be, but for helping me shape it into something I'm truly proud of.

Molly, you're a brilliant editor ... and I definitely did not curse quietly under my breath while reading your notes. Thank you for getting me.

And finally, to you—the fans. Thank you for being creeps. You've given me more than I ever imagined.

About the Author

Darcy Michael is an accomplished actor and joyfully neurodivergent comedian. Along with his husband, Jeremy Baer, Darcy entertains millions on his viral social media accounts. Find him at online @thedarcymichael. Darcy and Jer's sold-out 2023 comedy tour "No Refunds" has been adapted into a stand-up special and is the subject of the documentary *Happily Ever Laughter*. In 2024, *No Refunds: The Album* reached number one on North American comedy charts. Darcy and Jer live on Vancouver Island, Canada with their golden retriever, Yuma (@yumadog). For news and tour updates, visit darcyandjer.com.